# Securing Serenity in Troubling Times

## Living One
## Day at a Time

## Lawrence M. Ventline

This Dedicated to....
Molly Ann Bish...

Faith is more dark than light. Faith is
an illumined darkness, however.
Just enough to keep walking in a
world bursting with terror and
trauma. That glimmer gets me through it all,
providing a path shimmering
with hope.

# About The Author

C hoosing ministry over a career in medicine, Motown native, teacher, pastor and psychotherapist Lawrence Matthew Ventline of Detroit, is former executive director of the ecumenical Michigan Coalition for Human Rights, and, longtime religion columnist for The Detroit News. He received the 1997 Human Rights Award of the City of Detroit. He holds a Doctor of Ministry (D.Min.) from St. Mary's Seminary and University in Baltimore, Maryland. His doctoral thesis is "The Witness Value of the Visit of John Paul II to Detroit: Its Meaning and Message." Currently, Father Ventline is founding director of Care of the Soul and Companions, a pastoral household of spirituality and counseling with group guidance and individual direction for the People of God no one else may want to meet or care to provide therapy.

# Contents

# Foreword

*S*ecuring Serenity in Troubling Times: Living One Day at a Time tells tales that are so simple with human anecdotes that run throughout the pages. Acceptance, terror and and tips for coping with trauma are offered the reader.

It is a book about relationships, about people. Not those who are active on the world stage. Ordinary people. Father Lawrence Ventline's own family of brothers and sisters and parents, nine altogether, weave through this work. There are the people he meets in his life as a parish priest, counselor, spiritual advisor, neighbor and friend.

His tales and tips for attaining serenity are wrapped in the prayer of Detroit theologian Reinhold Niebuhr's popular Serenity Prayer used in countless self-help and Twelve Step spirituality groups. It is easy for me to recall with him the streets and neighborhoods, factories and schools, multicultural environment and all the vibrant life of Detroit the last couple of decades.

The stories are so very human. But there is always a presence of God in them because Fr. Ventline tries to live that presence himself and all that he experiences in his own humanity, for the events and people necessarily include an active awareness that God belongs and is part of everyone and everything in our life. Without realizing it immediately, we discover as we read these stories that we are being provided with spiritual guidance and nourishment. Evergreen hope is here.

Sometimes, I am sure, we all need explicit and very straight forward spiritual direction. But for an easy and gentle intrusion for achieving serenity in troubling times we could not find anything much better than connecting with people and encounters and issues Larry Ventline writes about. As we read, we find ourselves moving with him into rich spiritual reflections.

St. Theresa's prayer resounds in the readings put forth: "Let nothing disturb thee, nothing affright thee; all things are passing God never changes. Patient endurance attaineth to all things; who God possesseth in nothing is wanting; alone God sufficeth."

A posture of acceptance as told within by Father Edward Popielarz in his notes from a class in acceptance ring true for serene living. Issues of life and death, war and peace, suffering and dying and rising along with means of coping with fear are found within the stories. Quiet stillness and its importance for renewal and transformation are highlighted here. Action and contemplation go hand in hand.

I hope that many people manage to discover this book. They will not only enjoy the time they spend reading it, but the stories will illumine and help them discover their roots, new relationships, quiet reflections and a serene Spirit in troubling times today as they live each day fully.

Bishop Thomas J. Gumbleton, D.D.
Detroit, Michigan

# Introduction

Gripped by indifference, passivity, numbness, denial, dis-ease, and addiction, less and less hope envelopes a culture filled with fear in these troubling times in need of securing serenity. Our own "best" thinking finds us in a mess of international terror and trauma. Internally, rocked by corporate and church scandals and mismanagement, further deterioration is evident in the poor health of this Nation, and the state of its soul.

Lost in our own devices, Albert Einstein's challenge to bring new thinking to resolve old problems will alone ease the anxiety and Divine Disconnect strangling the soul of America.

Taking less time for stillness, exercise and recreation for our own wellbeing and health, we fail to admit of a culture of denial and addictive living. We don't even know that we don't recognize that we are numbed in paralysis in need of a great awakening that attunes us afresh to God again.

Unsure of our footing, unanchored in what Paul Tillich calls the Ground of all Being, we stray and stumble in escalating rates of self-destruction, lacking self-caring. Wide awake we need to be anew with new eyes, enlarged hearts, and fresh solutions to decade old dilemmas corroding the common soul, including domestic terror told of Molly Bish within.

The Divine Physician's prescription for securing serenity in troubling times clearly calls for a dose of tried and proven Twelve Step spirituality with "conscious contact" with the ultimate Tale Teller who weaves in and out of our struggles, rejection, abandonment, stillness, journaling, accepting, dying, courage, wisdom, and peace.

Living one day at a time, moment by moment in the gift of the Present, thawing the dulled, and indifference driving our lives requires awakening from the slumber of soulless lives.

Like Jonah the Prophet of the Hebrew Scriptures, who is transformed in the belly of a whale, with him we also need to be spit ashore in that inner initiation emerging in the Light as a new woman and man.

Competing to be the General Manager of the universe has futilely and finally failed us, leaving us in the grip of fear, with terror lurking around every corner, in each one's pockets, in so many hearts. Like midwives Shiprah and Puah (Exodus 1), who let the oppressive Pharaoh go his way and do his thing, we need to allow the Divine Healer to release us from a culture of death. Midwifing the abundant life of Jesus Christ in Detroit theologian Reinhold Niebuhr's (1892-1971) Serenity Prayer is the gift that wraps around the tales told within, and the hope-filled reflections written over a couple of decades for companions on the journey.

"If only I could never open my mouth. . .until the abstract idea had reached its highest point — and had become a story," shouts the boss in Zorba the Greek by Nikos Kazantzakis. We are a people "story hungry." Filling the void in our soul are transforming and tender tales and tips that will find you cozying up in your favorite easy chair or sitting by the fireside enjoying one or two.

Lawrence M. Ventine, D.Min.
Sterling Heights, Michigan

# The Serenity Prayer

God Grant me the serenity to accept the things
I cannot change;

Courage to change the things I can; and
Wisdom to know the difference –

Living one day at a time;
Enjoying one moment at a time;
Accepting hardships as the pathway to peace;
Taking, as He did, this sinful world
as it is, not as I would have it:
Trusting that He will make all things
right if I surrender to His Will;
That I may be reasonably happy in this
life and supremely happy with Him
forever in the next. Amen.

—Reinhold Niebuhr

# CHAPTER ONE

# *God, Grant Me the Serenity...*

## A Wordy World in Need of Silence

Ours is a wordy world. The space around us is filled with words that are whispered and words that are screamed; harsh words; gentle words; words that vie for our attention and words that seek to sell something fast. There are flashing words on the expressways and flickering words on neon signs that fly out at us everywhere.

The absence of words makes us nervous and anxious. Immediately, we want to fill up the empty spaces of silence in our lives. Comfort with silence is not our favorite pastime. We hear words in speeches and sermons, in lectures, and on television, only to conclude: Words! They are just words, words, words, words, and more words. Words said without silence are words without power!

The Taoist philosopher Chaung Tzu said, "The purpose of words is to convey ideas. When ideas are grasped, the words are forgotten. Where can I find a man who has forgotten words? He is the one I would like to talk to."

Silence teaches us to speak words wisely. It prompts us to refrain from abuse of words. Silence reminds our worlds of the value of words that have lost their meaning through overuse. Silence suggests that words are vehicles to put us in touch with ourselves and others. But, when they fail to achieve that end, they are simply words that flee fast from any semblance of silence.

Then, they mock the motto: Silence is golden.

The power of silence is suggested in the Fifteenth Century story of the Egyptian desert fathers. "Three fathers used to go and visit blessed Anthony every year and two of them used to discuss their thoughts and the salvation of their souls with him. But the third always remained silent and did not ask him anything. After a long time, Abba Anthony said to him, "You often come here to see me, but you never ask me anything." The other replied, "It is enough to see you, Father."

In silence, I often say the words on a plaque that was given to me by a parishioner: *"Lord, fill my mouth with worthwhile stuff, and nudge me when I said enough."*

## Stillness is Healing

Spirituality is about breathing God "in" and "out." Spirituality is an "inside" job, very close to one's heart in a world caught up on the "outside," emphasizing performance, function and "doing." Attending to the interior of one's life with God in the inner depths gives rise to heightened hopes for the active life. What kills is the frozen heart born of busyness and fatigue.

Mother Teresa observed that when one fills up on things, the person leaves little room for God. Emptying one's self of much means releasing distractions that keep us from the center. Disciplined praying moments are the only remedy for a heart turned from God.

Emptiness is what M. Scott Peck, M.D., notes is the third stage in forming community. After a "pseudo" community where one sets his or her "best foot" forward, followed by a chaos that aligns sides "for" and "against," the self-emptying process is realized as the only alternative to harmony in one's heart. The heart's peace and unity finally tires of tried and tested options that only leave one unsatisfied, hungry, and deprived, even cold.

There is little priority in our society, schools, churches, and communities "within" in our own worlds. The demand for such stillness can frighten the "busy" body, disquieted by the active life. Yet, unless more time, energy and efforts are placed on the traditional value of silence and solitude, little will be offered by our Catholic systems to satisfy a God-starving, dysfunctional society. We will only continue to "do" with little regard to "be."

Mentors who witness such pauses to ponder are the need of the day, as has always been true in our story. Clearing away the obstructions will be unpopular, strongly resisted, and dubbed "useless" by man. Yet, being "useless" before God in a "fix-it" society is the option worth holding high. Such stillness is healing. We will all be better for it and, a little less noisy and more knowing of the will of God. Quiet, please!

## Be Still

"Be Still." She said those words often. My teacher would command silence whenever she used them in school.

The story is told of the man who sat in the last pew of the church for fifteen minutes each day without exception. Curious as to what he would do during that time, the church caretaker finally asked him: "Why do you come here every day and sit here with your hat on your head and your pipe in your mouth?"

Uplifting his head, the man said in a gentle way: "I come here to look at my God while my God looks at me!

Stillness. In our time it is soothing as it silences the hurried and hectic pace of an advanced and busy age. Stillness shatters chaos and calms one's self. It is redeeming and healing. It is quieting. It is necessary even in our independence and drive toward individualism. Stillness sends us back into the lives of others to hear them and to listen to their cry. Stillness is strengthening. It prompts our best foot forward after careful reflection. Stillness is good.

## Seven Life Savers for Balancing the Boat

Maintaining balance in the boat of life requires the skills of an artist, the heart of Jesus Christ, and a body willing to "be" more than to "do" in a quick fix society. Seven life savers for balancing the boat include:

1. **Powerlessness** — The ability to recognize that the open, humble, empty, and poor in Spirit attitude has a power of its own. With the grace of God, we stop playing the so-called "power game" of trying to own and control others. Ever so slowly we come to admit that our behavior in thought, word and deed has become distorted and unmanageable, creating conflict in self and others. The false self that was formed years ago to defend self from those who shamed us finally falls to the truth that the true self emerges only in my powerlessness.

2. **Priorities** — The willingness to set limits, boundaries and God's vision and purpose as the way to peace. What do I want to do this day for the Lord, myself, others, and society? Name your intentions for the day or week. How I spend the time God has blessed me with will help in setting priorities. Review the way I live each day and reset personal and familial goals. List them.

3. **Personality and Principles** — The way I take personal inventory each day firmly believing and being a daughter or son of God who is very much loved will determine whether I am an optimist or a person who weighs heavy with the burdens I place upon my shoulders daily. Do I practice the principles of the Gospel that invite me into the more abundant life? Do I smile often? Is my personality pleasing to myself and others? Strive always to be personal with others, ever sharing the deep recesses of your heart with trusted friends and family.

4. **Play and Pause** — The ability to laugh, it seems to me, is when bonds get built among people and, in turn, ministry happens. Laughter and humor, **however,** cannot

happen without a pause from strenuous and hectic family and work-a-day weeks. Even a brief respite or a drive to the country or a walk in the woods may be sufficient to restore and refresh one's spirit. Organizing a neighborhood or family volleyball game is one way to insure a lot of laughs and much-needed diversion.

5. **Promotion** — Attraction to want the peaceful disposition one manifests in his or her life undoubtedly brings others to the fold, the parish, the social group or the bowling team. Twelve-step spirituality groups, such as Adult Children of Alcoholics (ACoA) or Alcoholics Anonymous (AA) are prime examples of attraction by promotion. Being for and with each other at home, church or the workplace is more central to the health of the nation than the economic growth of a country.

6. **Penitential Spirit** — A contrite heart always seeking renewal, reconciliation, recreation and recovery of a bruised spirit or community enables one to sleep at night with a clear conscience. The traditional examination of conscience with a specific follow-up action plan on healing relationships keeps conversion central in the Christian community.

7. **Praise and Prayer** — Giving praise to God in song or celebration of the Presence of God gives rise to a new way of living, loving laughing, crying and walking the Good News of Jesus. Like the other ways of balancing the boat, praise and prayer are non-negotiable means to insure healthy, wholesome sanctity, oftentimes robbed by an unwillingness to share, grieve, and celebrate the pain and the glory nestled in the secret places of each person's heart.

## Summary

Balancing the fragile act of life becomes easier when praise, prayer, play, pause, priorities, powerlessness, and the personal practice of the principles of truly being God's beloved enter center and front stage in each of our lives.

The Presence of God and one's own presence will illuminate any dimly-lit spirit lacking the glow of goodness and holiness that alone attracts and promotes the Christian message of Jesus who came to give us life and to give it more abundantly.

"I don't want people to give from the abundance," she tried to say to her TV audience. Mother Teresa wants us to share God's love with our very hearts and hands that touch the poor of our cities, the victims of AIDS, and the homeless hungry that scandalizes a nation filled with material wealth, technology and "know-how." She wants our selves, our substance, not our "extras," not our "left overs," but our "first fruits."

How easy it is for us to pay away our problems to others by throwing in a buck or two for someone else to touch human life with the love of the Lord. That's the consumer way of doing things. It excuses me. It gets me off the hook and salves my conscience. Mother Teresa didn't appear to want part of such giving with dollars. Reluctantly she gave Mr. Buckley an address. He smiled; her head humbled.

Over and over again, Mother Teresa spoke of the priority of stillness and prayer. "We pray four hours a day," she quipped. It went right by Mr. Buckley. He didn't know what to do with that response. Perhaps too simple for him, for our American capitalistic and consumer-oriented, money-making ways? "If prayer doesn't make money, why bother?" We seem to say.

Truth alone arises from the silence of being in the quiet presence of the Word, asserts the late Fr. Thomas Merton, the Trappist monk. Stillness alone will give birth to rearranging my own and this world's priorities to place the monk's simple and proven plea first to love, love, love, love, love. Amen.

*Serenity:*
*Fill me, come to me, join me*
*in communion and love.*
*As a gentle, cool breeze uplift me*
*and be the wind beneath my*
*worry, wonder, wandering and*
*war this day. Come, calm, come!*
*Calm and release anxiety and*
*doubt. Come, sweet serenity,*
*come and find a home in me!*

CHAPTER TWO

# *Accept the Things I Cannot Change*

## Pioneering Acceptance Way

He was born in Saginaw, MI, and early on in his childhood his family moved to Hamtramck, MI. Edward D. Popielarz, a professor at the Orchard Lake Schools the first half of his vocation, was a pastor also who gathered as many as a hundred participants each week for his class in acceptance since 1962.

Affectionately called, Father Pops, this boyhood pastor of mine, wrestled with his own demon of alcohol dependency, while helping others face addictive, destructive and harmful ways of disorders in loving.

"Acceptance" to Father Popielarz meant recognizing one's problem and seeking the answer in oneself while in communion with others. Every issue is a personal problem, Fr. Pops believed. Each problem is a love disorder. When someone does not know how to love, it is inevitable that he or she will develop a personal problem.

As with every shepherd and caretaker of souls, Pops taught people how to "love" and develop "empathy" to suffer with other people in their lives and situations.

What is it, then, that keeps one from loving well? A fear complex. People fear everything from the weather report, to losing their health or "nest egg," to losing their freedom and material security. "A loss in having, is a gain in being," Fr. Pops said often in his acceptance class. A fire destroys a home, for example, and a family huddles together in a hotel room for days. They reacquaint themselves with one another. What they "have" in their home is gone forever. What they "gain" now is "being" with each other anew. They connect again in relationship.

Couples may be threatened by each other, and seek to control the other. The fear may be so great one is afraid to risk giving and allowing the other to be free, and so one tightens the reins on the other, Pops believed.

In high school, I remember Fr. Popielarz, instructing me: "If I do not like something about you, I accept it and by accepting it, I create a climate of hope that you may change." Hoping one changes is superior to "expecting" one to change. Hope is open to freedom for the other. Expecting the other to reform is controlling, demanding, or requiring something of the other.

Want happiness? Pursue freedom, creativity and empathy, Fr. Pops recommended.

Elsewhere in Securing Serenity are the ingredients on learning to love well. Among the steps, first, one has to accept self and one's mess. One admits and owns that he or she has a problem. Accepting one's issue is key to healing it in time by the grace of God. Contact with others in the class flows into recognizing how one's problem emerged. Becoming an acquaintance of others with similar issues follows in the class in acceptance. Empathy rises through time. "Feeling with" another is a skill learned that helps one to be more accepting of another's position without becoming emotionally involved. That's empathy.

Practicing the principles of the class in acceptance, like prayer, cooking, playing cards, parenting, or running a marathon requires discipline and honesty, similar to twelve-step spirituality widely practiced throughout the world in its successful recipe for sobriety and wholesome wellbeing. Father Pops was "fresh air" for this high schooler, and, today, the skills he taught me are effective in relationships that require continual vigilance and growth. His skills secured a semblance of serenity for me.

## Toppled Trade Towers

Hello Terror,
My old friend,
I'm here to talk
to you again!

9/11, 2001, New York City, Ground Zero where my pilgrimage
began for a week of service to a broken people. I ache and wonder
how I will help. I am so sad to see man's inhumanity to man. It is
unbearable. It is so heavy. With God's help, I will serve. I will pray
with survivors and visitors to this latest shrine of ashes in the Big
Apple.

Healing such heartache and hurt takes time and tears.

Your impact, O Terror, and, your devastation destroys the Twin
Towers. Sacred ground survives the tumble. The putrid smell of
electrical fires and burning flesh fills my nostrils
these days as the Long Island Railroad carries me to this awful
and holy shrine. In the subway to the train, here is a world of frenzy
and fear. God, come by here. Kum Ba Ya, my Lord.

The sacred makeshift memorial recalls the memory of family,
friends, co-workers and acquaintances who vanished in the pulver-
izing heat and thunderous collapse of burning beams and broken
bodies. How much can a heart break open, I thought. I feel as
though my heart blew up and then again it burst a thousand times.

You, O Terror, are a six-foot-high pile of debris comprised of
human life. That life will rise again from the ashes, O terrible
Terror! Tears flood my face and I can stand no more the horror of it
all. Kneeling, I pray. Getting up from the wall of flowers, notes and
photos, I go to the church to sit. I calm down. I get myself together.

Hope is evergreen, O Terror! Hope will see us through the
plumes of fire and smoke that stained the morning sky that fateful
9/11. Dust and dirt from the fireball flames fill my eyes now. They
weigh me down with a heavy heart. Visitors look so afraid. Only
silence speaks now. Volumes shout in the sacred silence all about
me. It is too much for a human heart to bear.

Etched in my journal: December 11-18, 2001. Tired and tried I return by train to Bohemia. Father Louis Reuss hosts me at St. John Nepoumocene Church where I stayed on weekends in 1973 when I was an intern at Central Islip State Hospital in chaplaincy training. It is so good to rest a while away from the ache of bodies blown and burned instantaneously that fateful morn. Fr. Reuss loves life and laughs. A grand host and good shepherdly pastor, I cherish his wisdom and joy!

Hope will see me through the Holy Days of Christmas. Here is your sting, O Terror, but where is your victory? Holiday hope will soar. Light lives. Darkness is overcome.

God, I know we cannot contain Terror without you and your Truth. You are the path to life. Help us to see your light.

May I help to stop the violence and bring your Peace. Amen.

## A Modern Prayer for These New Times

The Lord bless you and keep you! The Lord's face shine upon you, and be gracious to you! The Lord look upon you kindly and give you peace! Numbers 6:22-28

A prayer for a new time: Good God, in this new time let me be a blessing in a world that seems so often to be bombed out of its mind. Help me to set sail amid streams that set straight a world beset by war and worry. Show me, Lord, the way that works right and wonderful in your sight. Give me, Lord the vision for the "extraterrestrial" — for gentleness and goodness, for truth and triumph.

Help me to arm myself in love, enabling me to let down the arms and arsenals that mock your mind and majesty. In this new time, Lord, bless people sleeping in city streets, people in refugee camps, people who have lost their homes to natural disaster, or to the human tragedy of war or loss of work. In this new time, guide us to learn how, when and how much you ask us to give so that all people on this earth may eat decently. Bless the hungry and bless those who feed them.

I beg your blessing on the wife whose husband has died; on the man whose wife has died; on children with no parents; on people torn by divorce, alienation, and misunderstanding; on people who have lost their best friend, a sister, a brother, a hero.

Lord, we thank you for being healthy enough to be able to enter this new time. Strengthen those suffering sickness and injury. Most of all, Lord, bless those in prison, people far away from their home-land, young soldiers at lonely outposts, and in the midst of battle; people who work for our safety, and security, and the peacemakers.

Lord, we beg your forgiveness and ask your help now that we have the knowledge and the things that can destroy the air we breathe, the things that can harm the land we walk, the things that can poison all our food and water; the things that can kill all crea-tures, including us, your people. Help us to learn what we must do with our horrible inventions so that the peoples of this earth will not be troubled by either madness or mistake. Amen

## We're All Doing Time

We're all doing time, aren't we, when imprisoned in fear, held hostage by that fear, gripped by it whether it's a weather report telling of more rain and other bad news, or, afraid of rejection or ridicule. Many prophets and saints were jailed, including St. Paul. St. Paul accepted his plight, however, and it made all the difference in the world for him.

As Americans and other foreigners in Iraq, including a Korean are being beheaded, I shudder at the silence of our government and the media. The media obsesses on stories when it wants to, but when humans are being decapitated, I hear only silence from them. What gives?

We're all doing time. When anyone is held hostage, we're all doing time. Sacred Scripture reminds that when one suffers all suffer in their ache. Has that changed in our culture? Families of those jailed helplessly worry for the detainee. Panic stirs some.

The hidden world of prisons gets as grueling as Iraq's Abu Ghraib. No need to go any further than Michigan's lock-ups that have taxpayers paying $1.8 billion a year.

One prisoner wrote this to me: "You could take a shower to try to relax and wash away the pain inside only to find out I could not get a towel. You had to have a written order for everything yet not allowed a pencil. I stayed in my cell and cried. It was like being a lion in a cage. Their dog food chased away my appetite. It was very lonely."

More jails are being built. We're all doing time just to think that caging people will rehabilitate them.

## Who are Those Called the Free?

The free — who are they? Rich, poor, landowners, or peasants? You? Me? Or, countries backed with military might? Free people hear the Jewish plea to "choose life" and they are free who embody what psychologist Carl Jung calls "something that lives and endures underneath the eternal flux." For Christians, the free are persons who live every life with the hope symbolized in the dying and rising of Jesus — the great liberator who loves all people.

They are free who break the chains that hold down the needy; who release those held hostage in the sin of greed that shows itself in oppressive and enslaving structures and systems in "Third World" cities of Detroit, New York, Chicago, El Salvador and Warsaw. The free are people who help others to walk with pride again, having been Each of us is free when we bind every wound, shelter the sick, share our many possessions with the poor, protect the innocent, challenge a mistaken arms race that robs the dispossessed of dignity, are compassionate with the bereaved, and unlock life paralyzed by the "isms" of race, age, and sex. The extent to which people are free rests in economic budgets that show whom and what we value. Although this task to free persons is done imperfectly and limitedly, nonetheless, for the free that is the focus of a lifetime's task.

That freedom was the hope of Mother Teresa of India, the violent-free living of Gandhi, Merton, Dr. Martin Luther King, Jr., Bishop Raymond Hunthausen, Pope John XXIII, and Bishop Thomas Gumbleton. When each of us is truly free, then we are heirs of life, liberty and the pursuit of happiness.

## Remember Those Who Have Fallen

The wall, war and wonder. All three come to mind this February 18. The date marks the anniversary of the death of my brother Lukas in Vietnam.

Friends, family, and survivors of the more than 58,000 Americans killed or missing in action in Vietnam, coupled with intentions for all who mourn the loss of loved ones in all our warring moments, will gather to pray at Mass. I'm sure we'll talk about the national Vietnam Veterans' Memorial in Washington, D.C., the black granite wall that shines with hope and cuts into the earth within sight of the Washington Monument. And, we'll wonder again how the U.S. realized that it was losing a war it should not have been There will be discussion, I'm sure about the year 1968 – the year of riot and revolution, the year Richard Nixon was elected, when man orbited the moon for the first time, when the Viet Cong launched the Tet offensive. Dr. Martin Luther King, Jr. was assassinated as was Robert Kennedy a few months later. The year 1968 was the year I was called to the phone at St. Mary's College, Orchard Lake, to hear my sister say, "He's gone!" February 18 was the day before my parents' wedding anniversary.

It was a year of shatterings, indeed. Starvation plagued Biafra. The American intelligence ship, Pueblo, was seized. Some say 1968 marked the end of the civil rights movement, paved the start of the women's movement and stirred environmental consciousness. The wall, war and wonder keep coming back.

At his funeral Mass, we were told my brother brought us one step closer to peace. I wanted to believe that. Countless moments of energy find me struggling to accept the mystery of God in misery of war among peoples.

The telephone rang shortly after the morning Mass back in 1982 when I was pastor of St. Christine's Parish, Detroit. Parishioners had arranged to fly me to Washington for the dedication of the wall. I was excited, to say the least. The late afternoon flight, amid turbulent weather, could send me, hopefully, into putting some more closure on a war that still makes me wonder years later.

Family who lived in nearby Washington would meet me at the

airport. They would be holding yellow flowers so I could identify them. We met and rushed to the cathedral where the names of all the war dead were being announced. I would get to say my brother's name. I followed a crippled vet who would read the name of his best friend who didn't make it. Like his, my voice quivered.

It was pouring outside. The rain wouldn't stop us from locating my brother's name on the stone. It was a sad place. It seemed like they were all buried there. It seemed like church and rite and a long litany of brothers and sisters in the Lord. The rain showered harder. My tears wed with the rain.

The names of those who died and those who remain missing are inscribed in the order they were taken from us.

With the help of green-jacketed vets, my brother's name was located. We prayed. It was good to be there. Friends who go to the Wall continue to give me photos of my brother's name. Starlight seems to shine on one. It is that light that gives hope. Therein, the mystery and the misery merge. So be it.

## The Voices of Conscience?

Doors keep shutting on human decency. Whether it's dogs, dye or tear gas staving off black people in South Africa's protest against segregated elections, and "white people's beaches only" signs, or the ugly scene at Auschwitz where a Carmelite convent has exploded into an international scandal just as the fiftieth anniversary of the Nazi war on Poland to start World War II was marked.

We must own again the civil rights battle of the sixties. All must unite against indecency to the dignity of peoples everywhere. A war on drugs has been declared. We're worried about our kid's addictions and the beepers some of them wear to school these days so that their dealers can have instant contact to their devilish habits. We tell the youngsters to say "no" to drugs and quickly send them off to fast-food store wages that don't work any more, since they've learned from mom and dad how the almighty buck has taken center stage and pushed God to the edge.

Adolescents are wise to that, too. They have learned the plan to make megabucks and they make them, legal or not, with jobs that fill their pockets with more than change.

Healing the earth seminars are finding a two-track collision course with Jesus' sermon on the mount to rid ourselves of the need to always be right, to be powerful, and to succeed at all costs and never fail.

Predictions hold that we will destroy ourselves in thirty seconds or thirty years, and we're currently working on both projects. Pollution of water with waste, oil, and garbage with no industrial toilet for such debris has become an international nightmare as we reject each other's ship loads of refuse into our harbors.

Where are the voices of conscience these days? Who will stand up and put an end to doors that keep shutting on human decency? Full active and conscious participation called for by the bishops of Vatican II may be our only alternative to an already bad situation. Heaven help us all.

## Pondering, Remembering, Still

Pausing, pondering, and remembering our war dead this Memorial Day. All the dead from the conflict told of in the Bible of the jealous Cain killing his brother Abel, to the World, Korean, Vietnam, Persian Gulf, Afghanistan, and Iraq wars and individual battles brewing about everywhere.

One in ten is dying of HIV-AIDS in Tanzania. There on that African continent children witness their parents die of this infectious killer disease that's willing to wipe out a people. I think of the children and recall the words of Norene Vest:

"Be full of care with everything entrusted to you. Everything you touch or see, everyone for whom you have responsibility, is to be viewed as something cherished by God, and thus to be cherished by you."

The admonition of the great physician Albert Schweitzer buoys from within me this Memorial Day:

"I cannot but have reverence for all that is called life. I cannot avoid compassion for everything that is called life. That is the beginning and foundation of morality."

Formally declared wars or not, conflicts range in this land's schools these days. Children shoot bullets about schoolyards. I remember young Kayla near Flint gunned down by a boy who didn't know anything about war in his fragile soul. Columbine High School's slaughter surfaces, also. More precious lives snuffed out in the richest land of the world, let alone a wealthy suburb of Denver, Colorado.

Oh, I pause and ponder this Memorial Day and wonder: Have we become powerless over violence in an undeclared war at home? Are we in denial that we seem helpless in this battle that reports murder of children as commonly as blowing one's nose?

I shed a tear for all the war dead this day, my brother Spec. 5 Lucas Ventline, included among the 58,000 slaughtered in Vietnam alone, excluding all the others who died and are dying in our countless conflicts.

Parades and processions mark this Memorial Day as last year and will next year. The will to remember is strong and unstoppable. That same will to silence the sounds of guns among our youngest citizens needs to match our Memorial Day tradition.

There is something healing in remembering our war dead. Tragically, there is something even more sad watching parents bury their bullet-shattered children.

We will remember this day. Let us not forget the "will" to stop added memories of names of others who will die of gunshot wounds after this year's parades, picnics and parties. From Tanzania to our shores of shining seas, life is too sacred to fail to remember.

**Wondering about War and My Warrior Brother Lukas 35 Years Later**

"I wish they'd stop calling it the anniversary of Roe Vs. Wade because it's a memorial," the physician across the table said with passion the other day over supper.

"You're right," I quipped back spontaneously between bites of my salad. Then he showed me Fr. Frank Pavone's, Resources for Clergy, including dilation and evacuation abortion (D & E) of a 23 week old baby in the womb and his or her own embattled war.

Yes, war is in the air, in the womb, on the battlefields, and in the minds of many these days. In fact, every year around February 18, my prayer and reflections turn more intensely to the Vietnam War's massacre of 58,000 Americans, let alone countless Vietnamese including innocent children and women, sad to say. It was this month in 1968 when I was a freshman at Orchard Lake St. Mary's College that an urgent call from my sister, Marcyanna, had me knowing it was about the demise of my brother Lukas in that war that President Lyndon Johnson's chief architect now calls a "mistake."

The good doctor was right on abortion and the memorial we mark each January 22nd. In turn, the memorial marking the death of so many in Vietnam, including my 23-year-old brother, is more apt a term than anniversary. He was the oldest of seven of us kids. I wonder what he would be doing today, 35 years later at 58 had he lived. An assembly line worker at the Chrysler Jefferson plant, he was 6'3" and one to look up to as my older brother who handed me his paper route and monument company jobs before he moved on to Chrysler's and then Vietnam, and his heavenly home due to fatal shrapnel wounds.

While with groups of Vietnam veterans twice yearly ever since my brother's death, I cringe at the stories they tell and the pain and tears in their eyes. War's trauma is obvious in their voices, the wounds of their souls. After all, we were meant to be lovers over warriors, God said.

War clouds over Iraq muster revisited attention to Pope John XXIII's 40-year-old vision "to all men of good will" in Pacem in Terries, Peace on Earth, the subject of Pope John Paul's World Day of Peace Message and of a message to journalists Jan. 24.

The way to peace, as John Paul summarizes the encyclical's teaching, "lay in the defense and promotion of basic human rights." Pope John XXIII was optimistic about peace. The United Nations and its Universal Declaration of Human Rights were key to his high hopes. Today, John Paul prays for peace, still, concludes that there may be times when war is not inevitable. John XXIII was unafraid to think "outside the box" in challenging leaders to new possibilities in lifting up human life's dignity.

A call to a Methodist pastor recently had him rattled by the thoughts of war. I heard it in his voice, his worry, his wonder. Turning to his own battle these days with cancer and the weariness caused by radiation treatment, he shouted with conviction and fire in his soul: "I tire of cerebral arguments about war, about exclusion of people, and the pain caused them by our lack of love. It's all about grace...I am who I am by the grace of God," he moaned.

Battles, battles everywhere, it seems these days. There is something about God's grace in the physician's war on abortion, the pastor's battle with cancer, and my own grief over war that snuffs out human dignity and life. Love really is the answer. It may be simple but war is hell and never to be entered as a lone country without the common good of our globe in mind as John XXIII and John Paul II remind us so well, let alone Jesus, the prince of peace, and Mary, queen of peace.

## An Alternative to Violence

I cringed each time the nonviolent and peaceful disciples of Gandhi were struck down. The spilling of blood always injures my sensibilities. All forms of violence and terror – from womb to tomb – turn my stomach. Violence waters my eyes. It doesn't do anyone any good, particularly our impressionable children. Every day youngsters view televised violence that makes destruction seem a natural part of society.

Gandhi — the great peacemaking Indian whose strategy of peace led to the liberation of India reminds us that violence is not the only way to resolve hostility. It awakens in me the need to work on this idea of peaceful co-existence. Jesus succeeded at such an approach. Dr. Martin Luther King, Jr. put it out there also. Thomas Merton prayed for it. Still all three died as victims of the violent ways they fought. But, they never lost their drive to be "gentle" men.

Gandhi's idea has been tried, tested, and found triumphant. It's a better way for us. And its time has come to give it a try today, tomorrow, and always. We'll all be better for it. No doubt about it. I'll be better for our children, most of all.

## Trauma Tips

You indeed, O God, give light to my lamp; you brighten the darkness about me. Psalm 18:29

Did you know that some darkness and pain are part of every person's path? The 1979 Nobel Peace Prize winner, Mother Theresa, confesses in her diary that at times she felt rejected by God, helpless and tempted to abandon her work caring for the poor and dying of India. Embrace the darkness.

Out of the depths I call to you, O Lord; Lord hear my cry! May your ears be attentive to my cry for mercy. Psalm 130:1-2.

Come to Me all who are weary and find life burdensome, and I will give you rest. -Jesus

## Facing Fear and Terror:
## Reminders for Coping

Seneca said that less informing and more reminding may be more of what we need.

We are alive and invited by God to enjoy the abundant life – always strive to be happy.

When we face fear and terror we don't have to follow the panic of the pack.

Just don't go there. Choose a fear-free life.

Others will try to instill terror and fear.

Choose not to let that paralyze you.

Don't allow feelings of fear to do your thinking.

Jesus says: Fear is useless – What's needed is trust.

Acknowledge the feelings of being afraid, and then let them go. Choose to feel something else.

Few of us know how to respond to fear and terror. Don't fill up on it, however.

Talk about your fear and feelings of terror.

Join a group to assist in facing fears. Don't go it alone.

No system is perfect. People do attempt to terrorize or dominate.

If nightmares about 9/11/01 or some other trauma unsettle you; consult a mental health professional.

When your heart is heavy, recognize the feelings of sadness, anger, and fear.

Accept and own your own experiences.

Times of terror and fear may cause intense emotions. You may be surprised at what you're feeling.

Follow a daily routine as much as possible. Pray, walk, eat well, sleep sufficiently, and have some fun also.

Laugh some – now, and later and tomorrow…Tell a joke. Be good to yourself, especially in the tough times.

Trust God. Think good thoughts – even for your enemies.

*Acceptance:*
*Saturate me and free me*
*that I may encircle all dealt*
*me in life.*
*O covenant of freedom, stir*
*within me the ability to embrace*
*pain, suffering, rejection, inclusion,*
*heartache and glad tidings.*
*Come, acceptance, come and*
*live in me now and always!*

# CHAPTER THREE

# ...Courage to Change the Things I Can, and....

## My Six Principles of Change

1) As I believe in the Real Presence and transubstantiation of the elements of bread and wine at Mass, I know that you can change when you believe it. When you believe it, you will see the change!

2) Give us this day our daily bread requires daily and ongoing commitment to change each day. This is more critical than the type of treatment proposed.

3) Brief commitments with possible relapses can change enduring habits (vices). Stay the course as Jesus did. Spend yourself for others.

4) Learning or unlearning life skills and vices can be the key to licking addictions. Now, go ahead and name the issues in your pilgrimage of life. All is possible with God (Sarah and Abraham).

5) Practice matters most. Treating recovery like a hotel to connect with when "I feel like it" will ensure you to keep the "old man" and "old woman" far from the new creation Paul speaks about. Have a mission. Follow up on goals. Practice, practice, practice! It works. Pray, pray, pray, at a definite time daily. Exercise daily at a scheduled time. Laugh and enjoy daily.

6) God lives in the relapses and valleys and seeming "failings" of

keeping my schedule of practicing. Start over. Brush off and commit to God, group and joy. Add a dash of positive posture and watch your attitude change. Be a transformer as Vatican II invites all believers, right where you are - at home, school, work, play, prayer...transform the earth with an aroma of Christ, a fragrance of Love.

St. John of the Cross and Teresa of Avila speak of *recovering* our original self God made us without strings and conditions. Remember 3 conversions: Purgative (take off masks, crawl); illuminative (insight, light goes on that God loves me as I am without strings, discover, walk); and Divine Union (running into arms of God, recovering through centering prayer daily, twice for 15-20 minutes soaking like a sponge God's love: "You are my beloved" (repeat, repeat, repeat)!

## Don't Hide Fears from God

In a hectic life, prayer can provide greater freedom. People can create freedom within themselves if they allow their thoughts and emotions to surface. Running and hiding one's feelings is unnecessary if one believes God is willing to receive them.

The constant discipline of presenting one's inner fears, concerns, and anxieties to God each day means saying: "Lord, I'm so angry with this person...I can't bear the situation I'm in. I don't even know if I believe anymore...I'm so confused...." Rather than running from such feelings, one can be freed by saying: "Here I am, Lord, in our presence. I know you are a loving God. I present to you all that is within me. Help me."

When one uses this method for ten minutes each day, a whole new way of living is experienced. Jesus hid nothing from His Father. He lived his life in the presence of His Father. He could say to His disciples: "You will be scattered...leaving me alone. And yet I am not alone, because the Father is with me."

Facing up to the feelings of life can free one to enjoy living. Prayer as a discipline means using the Bible, reading it, and using it like an icon...something to look at. Then I direct myself toward the picture or statement: "The Lord is my shepherd; nothing shall I fear." I put that image at the center of my attention and see my feelings and my confusion in the light of what the Lord is saying or doing in the Scriptures. Then the Lord becomes a real partner in a prayer conversation; and, I offer to God my total self and feel freedom again.

## A Better Attitude to Be Happy

"A person has to resolve to be happy," the lady said as she moved with pain in her hospital room, the victim of an automobile accident three weeks ago. That's my resolution for 1980 — to be happy," she said as she wondered what I would resolve to do in the New Year. Resolutions are quickly forgotten, I thought, and then I proceeded to suggest some specifics for myself.

I'm going to decide to accept all people; I may not approve of their behavior or agree with their opinions, but I can certainly try to accept them as creatures made in the "image and likeness of God," as affirmed in the first book of the Bible.

But, even before that, I will accept myself with my own limitations and shortcomings. My physical, mental and emotional make-up will find acceptance by myself. I will always find this humbling, yet calming. I will always try to keep before me an attitude of trust, hope and love for others and myself.

I won't try to change anyone because I know, realistically, I can't unless I get caught up in the power struggle, trying to own, manipulate, and control others. I will be gentle in my dealings with others. I'll stop thinking that a two-year-old or a ten-year-old should "grow up." I'll remember instead the words of Jesus: "Unless you become like a little child, you cannot enter the kingdom of heaven."

With Alexander Pope, I will shout: "To err is human; to forgive, divine." My values will center on "being" rather than on "having" people, places, or things. I'll relish the need to be a human being over the need to find happiness in unnecessary material things; or, in the drive for money, power or drugs, like alcohol.

Hallmarks of St. Paul will guide my every moment: love, joy, peace, patience, kindness, gentleness and self-control. I will try to be compassionate in my solidarity with others, that is, to be aware of the human sameness all people share, whether rich or poor, young or old, male or female, strong or weak.

I will try to hear each human being I talk with. I will try to enter as fully as possible into the joys, fears, and hopes of others, putting aside any artificial blockades that encourage distance, safety, and escape from the hurts of others. I will be led, perhaps, where I would rather not go, realizing that leading and loving is not founded on control but rather on trust. I will listen long to the word of God in the Bible, trusting its power to liberate self and others from poverty, injustice and violence when I am truest to that message. To be happily alive will be primary for every breathing moment God gives me this year – like the lady who prompted a resolution in the first place.

### Forgiveness Can Serve as a Liberating Lesson

Forgiveness creates its own rewards for those trying to master this quality. Pope John Paul II's magnanimity in forgiving his would-be assassin was demonstrated in dramatic example to a world that has yet to learn to forgive. Anyone who forgives knows that forgiveness liberates one from the entrapment of resentment, outrage and isolation. The forgiver knows the reward of putting an end to the repetition of wrongdoing in one's life. Like the forgiving father in the gospel story in which he forgives his extravagant son for his squander and senseless living, magnanimity and mercy know their own place.

Much like Alexander Pope who said, "To err is human: to forgive is divine," one has to admit that forgiveness assures people that they can be redeemed and the darkness and disorder can be met with more sane and decent responses. Feuding spouses know the binding quality of forgiveness. They know the rich reward of happier lives when forgiveness gives way to the oneness they desire in untiring efforts to forgive.

John Paul – like Gandhi and Jesus — refuses to employ the world's vengeance mentality for "an eye for an eye and a tooth for a tooth." He knows that such cold-heartedness can only leave the world frozen in bitter revenge. Although it is only fashionable for a few, forgiveness is catching on as that quality needed in our time for survival. Psychotherapists agree that it's the healthier way to live a more wholesome existence. All of that is good news in a world in search of better ways to settle differences.

## Forgiving When Forgiveness is Hard

Forgiving is good for one's health. The heart pumps better.

When I decide to forgive someone, my heart sighs with joy and relief. Sweet.

To err is human; to forgive is divine. – Alexander Pope

I must have peace of mind as my goal – not trying to change or hurt the other person.

Until I learn to forgive, the Middle East, major conflict and I will never heal.

Father, forgive them, for they know not what they are doing. – Luke 23:34

Whatever you bind on Earth will be bound in heaven; and, whatever you loose on Earth will be loosed in heaven. – Matt. 18:18

To forgive – I accept the situation and I decide to let go.

I bring the eyes of God into my unforgiving heart and ready my heart for God's touch.

I let God's eyes fall upon the one I can't forgive. I see the love in God's eyes for my "enemy." I change.

Chains are lifted from my enslaved and choking heart when I forgive.

As Ghandi said – a tooth for a tooth and an eye for an eye will leave us all unable to see.

Forgive us our sins as we forgive those who sin against us. – Jesus

How often do I forgive? Always. All ways.

Anger and forgiveness will eat me alive – from the inside out.

Forgiveness, like building one's self-esteem and being happy – these are inside jobs.

If I want forgiveness I must give it – go on now – give.

For-give-ness.

Giving it to get it.

Where there is forgiveness, there is freedom. Free at last!

As forgiveness is extended to another, I must not forget to forgive self.

Who haven't I forgiven?

Have I forgiven myself for things I did? _____Yes _____No

Forgiveness is a fragrance I cannot buy. It is an aroma pervading me.

## Some Ways to Restore Decency Today

If today is an average day for deaths, many people will die from handguns. Imagine for a moment that you're a 14-year old boy in a major city talking about a TV sitcom with your friends on a street corner. You repeat a line and everybody laughs, perhaps a little too loudly for some; nevertheless, it's the way teens roar. Suddenly, you see fear fill the eyes of a passerby just then. Save Our Sons and Daughter's (SOSAD) Clementine Barfield advocates impassioned leaders.

What do you think? You think the man walking past doesn't enjoy even the thought of you. Picture also the scene of James Brady with the late former President Ronald Reagan as the press secretary falls to the ground, another handgun victim maimed for life. Then, think of movies, music and books that have become an unchallenged mode of teaching our children that violence, human indecency and war is the way to solve our personal and international conflicts. Watch a movie like the *Silence of the Lambs* and weep when witnessing a serial murderer who skins his victims. Read American Psycho and weep some more.

Now, act surprised at the report by Senate Judiciary Committee, claiming that the United States is the "most violent and self-destructive nation on earth." A record number of robberies, rapes, and assaults led the pack in the United States, a murder rate more than twice that of Northern Ireland, four times that of Italy, nine times England's and eleven times Japan's. Violence and abuse is a "fix" this Nation can no longer afford to deny as an issue we refuse to face as destructive.

Call it the new world order, but call it disorder. Call it murder mainstream as a way of life in America that mocks the very message of the Gospel of Jesus Christ upholding the dignity of the human person. Thou shall not kill! Imagine alternatives.

## How to Journal

More and more people these days are turning to the pen to etch their hearts' yearnings and aches as an effective way of therapy. Writing down one's thoughts, feelings, and emotions to a single passage in the Scriptures, for example, affords one the healing benefit to commune with the Lord, to focus one's scattered being, and to center one's life on stillness for ten to twenty minutes daily.

Research of Dr. James Pennebaker of Southern Methodist University in Texas demonstrates improvement in immune functions, lower blood pressure, reduced heart rate and an enhanced psychological condition among those who participated in a writing experience. For Pennebaker, the technique is simple: "Focus on issues you are living with, experiences you find yourself thinking or dreaming about too much of the time. Find a place where you can be undisturbed. Let go and write about your deepest emotions for fifteen or twenty minutes at a time. The only rule is to write continuously during that time. You don't have to worry about grammar; write just for yourself, as though you were going to throw this away."

Writing therapy helps people organize unmanageable feelings, making them more manageable, thus diminishing mental stress, according to Pennebaker. Besides providing the opportunity to capture in print one's fears, future longings, praises, or petitions, the commitment to journaling provides a healthy forum in which one can glean emerging themes or patterns of behaviors over a period of time.

## Begin with Trust

How does one begin to journal? What are some ways to take the pen to hand and get off dead center to write? Trust is the key. Without a willingness to trust one's inner self, coupled with the confidence to let flow what freely surfaces, journaling will be a chore and an effort that it is not meant to be.

In one's journal, to give an example, unless trust is present, the following entry would not be noted: "How I need the Spirit to 'let loose' in my life those areas that drive me to work, seek approval, and blunt my feelings in my busy days. It is critical that I 'let go and let God.'" To return to one's journal after an absence could not occur if one's trusting attitude and assurance that it's okay to miss a day is not present. Writing in the first person, as evidenced in the entry below may enhance the importance of keeping a journal: "I missed you a few days. I guess I needed to in order to appreciate you more than ever now and how important you are to me."

## Self –Disclosure

A willingness to be vulnerable and transparent in disclosing one's heart is vital to the process. Knowing that each entry is made with the assurance that only I will have access to it promotes blunt honesty: "Sometimes I feel like a sad song and all alone in life. My heart breaks this morning, Lord, because it falls short of enlarging in charity for others so often."

In the Marriage Encounter movement, putting the "pen to hand" is referred to as the "hot pen" method in which the person effortlessly lets the pen flow with whatever comes to one's mind as she or he writes continuously without stopping. Such a method promises disclosure of even one's deepest emotions and thoughts.

## Twelve Ways To Journal Tales

1. Read passages of Scripture and then reflect for a few minutes quietly. Employing a passage or two from the daily lectionary of the Mass is recommended, given the numerous meditation books available today to be used as resources (such as Living Faith, Daily Catholic Devotions by Creative Communications for the Parish, 10300 Watson Road, St. Louis, MO. 63127). Then write a response from the heart, using the "hot pen" method. Another use of Scripture may be to think of

your favorite saying of Jesus in the New Testament. Ponder that passage for awhile. When you can no longer contain the favorite words of the Master, write a response to Jesus.

2. Write on your moods. Review the events or encounters of the last day or two. Inscribe the predominant feelings (mad, sad, glad, or scared). Name the mood. Own the mood by admitting to it as part of your life. Finally, tame the mood by suggesting in writing how to cope with it.

3. Recall highlights of the day. Pool important happenings in the day and respond to them in your journal. Color the feelings that accompany the significant moments with oranges, greens, and purples. Identify the feelings (joy, exhilaration, sadness, anger) that go with the event.

4. Address the future. Write a letter to the Lord expressing what you would like to see in your life this month.

5. Reconcile in the journal. List persons you need to forgive. Pause to write a prayer for them. Write about how those persons are present with you and the Lord. How is the Lord present to you and the others? Is there something about the Lord's gestures, smile, gaze or arms that are reassuring? Write down any shortcomings or faults. Answer the question: How forgiving am I of myself?

6. Put yourself in the hand of God. Imagine yourself in God's hand and feel the experience through trusting God's carrying you through turbulence as on the sea. Write down or use crayons to capture the experience.

7. Write a letter to a fear you have. Lovingly, accept the fear and let it go. For example, write: Dear Rejection: I'm so scared when I think of being abandoned, forgotten, rejected or told I'm no good. I hand you over to the Lord. I am letting you go right now, right here.

8. Speak to another person or others. In monologue or dialogue with a person(s) you find it most difficult to address tell why it is difficult to speak to them.

9. Promises to the Lord. Write down what you want to do to improve your relationship with the Lord.
10. Speak to the Lord. Write down whatever is uppermost in your heart at the moment. Visualize the Lord, however you imagine him, as being right there with you as you speak and record the encounter in your journal.
11. Petitions. In a column note the things you need from the Lord for yourself, family, neighborhood, city, state, or oppressed country.
12. Praise. Note recent experiences that gave you peace, joy, a sense of calm. Write down the praise you felt in your heart when you met the Lord in a daughter, a son, a handicapped child, a beggar, a boss, yourself or an elderly person.

## Conclusion

Monitor your relationship with the Lord and others as you pen these ways of keeping a journal. Observe how your day may or may not be different using any or all of these techniques. Keep your journal for some years to compare your growth. Most of all, experience the healing touch that writing produces. Praise God.

### Soothing Light of Summer

Summer's official entry June 21, undoubtedly beamed sunlight and soothing rays so easily taken for granted. There's something about this season's sunlight, daylight, starlight, and moonlight that is readily embraced.

Humans prefer light over darkness. People go to extremes to push out dreaded or depressing darkness with light lamps to sun the seasonal affective disorder of the reported thirty-five million Americans in the height of winter's blanket of dark. Light is in. Dark is out. No doubt about it. We've heard them all: It is better to light one candle than to curse the darkness." Singers Peter, Paul and Mary chime, "Don't let the light go out!" "Light and lively yogurt." Coors Light." George Bush's "1,000 Points of Light." Motel 6's,

"We'll leave the light on for you."

I would give almost anything this summer for the light it will take to garner sufficient solutions to overcome the violence in our day that has become the way of almost the first resort for so many people. God knows how firearms kill thousands of Americans annually, as compared to only a handful in countries such as Japan or England. There are just too many guns in this nation. Children hardly begin to see the light of day in their growing years when they experience violence as the American way on TV, in the streets, in the schools, and even in our quick-to-shoot approach with countries that appear to be a threat to us or our lifestyle.

This summer I will pray daily for a little light blessed with some enlightened discussions of the finest minds we have in this community, including victims and rehabilitated perpetrators. Shedding some light to counteract a culture of violence will be a dangerous challenge to a system that thieves on a "macho man" menu of guns and fists and bombs to settle differences. Our children deserve better. We all do.

This dilemma has to be confronted now by courageous and prophetic leaders and parents not unlike the martyrs of the early Christian era who died for hard truths. The common good demands that decent folks convene for conversations that will craft solutions to harness the runaway train of spiraling violence and wars. I want to join others to shed some shared light – sunlight of hope – on this subject. We will all lose otherwise, and, only give way to more darkness.

## Quest for Quietude in 2005

One's best thinking gets him or her in a mess: Acting out anger, using drugs, conflict, resentment, accidents, indiscretions, violations of the law, for a few examples. New management with different thinking than that which put one in the mess has to be engaged. Albert Einstein said that, reminding people that the same thinking that caused a problem cannot be used to solve the same issue. Yet, how easy it is to resort to that same flawed reasoning in hopes that a better solution emerges. Not so!

So often one identifies with his or her thinking, his or her mind. "I think, therefore I am," the philosopher Descartes said. Am I not more than my thoughts, more than my mind, beyond reasoning? Am I not much more than "racing thoughts" and internal dialogue, more than constant chatter that locks one into his or her worries, fears, and frenetic pace? Look only to the mess and admit that the best thinking one gave to a problem got him or her into it. There has to be another way.

Year 2005 may well be the year of quietude. This new time may well be a moment for being under new Management in daily affairs. After all, as they say in the twelve steps of Alcoholics Anonymous – the Western world's contribution to spirituality, far different from the East's quieting of the mind readying it for meditation and "communio" with God. When the sober men rose from their addicted states of alcoholism and stopped drinking, they confessed in their first of twelve ways how they quit: We admitted that we were powerless over alcohol. Our lives had become unmanageable. They changed their thinking. They behaved differently then. Sober! Awake! Conscious! Numb no more! Transformed! Securing serenity in their troubled times.

Used today in countless church basement and parish halls by recovery groups of all sorts (narcotics, food, anger, gambling, sex, nicotine, dependency, work, to name a few obsessive problems) the 12 steps are a gift to those who practice this art of living sober lives. In fact, Step 11 calls for "conscious contact" with God. Being quiet is the lone way to still the mind, free it of constant thinking, and going deeper into one's soul where God is finally allowed to manage one's daily affairs.

### A Checklist Compass for Living a Moral Life

"How do I know I'm living my life well?" I was asked. Knowing that this rather short question would entail a longer answer, I invited the curious believer to sit down for a chat. The eyes of this middle-aged parent of three teens told it all. The gentleman wanted some direction. I was impressed.

You must understand that the person is a Christian after a

deeper life than that of a superficial seeker of money alone in life. Clearly, a man of depth here, I thought.

Traditionally, an examination of conscience at the beginning or end of the day is an excellent way of mapping one's progress in the moral life. That is, have I deliberately done wrong to another person? Have I transgressed against my God or my neighbor? Cheated? Been unfaithful? Trampled? Have I forgotten that the goods of health, happiness, and fortune are blessings from God to be shared? Do I speak well of others; or, do I gossip and degrade. Am I a person of life (or death)? Am I enthusiastic?

Can I readily detect what my life is about? Is it related to Christ or a power greater than me? How do I know myself? What are my peak moments, crises, life story? Can I share this story with another? Can I draw my story with crayon or sculpt it in clay or write it out?

What in me is a blessing to others? What is damaging in me? Are others better for me for my presence, laughter, humor, work, play or conversations?

Do I really connect with God? Do I pray? By myself? With others? Does prayer provide a context for our eating together, asking this question at meals at home or in a restaurant: For what are we thankful today? Then each person says a phrase, naming what he or she is grateful for to family, friends, and God.

Do I take time to be familiar with God's Word"? Is there a Bible character like myself? Is it Job, for example, on the brink of despair? Hosea married to the unfaithful Gomer? Elizabeth who welcomes Mary with grand hospitality?

Can I be still or am I always running, working, achieving, doing? Is genuine leisure a reality? Do I take time to reflect alone? With others? How is my life's work making the world a better place? Do I share my hopes and frustrations with others? Am I happy?

After we talked, the man seemed to walk more confidently, almost dancing his way out of my office. I handed him a copy of this check list for the moral life."

***Courage:***
*Instill in me virtue and strength*
*to see red rage at my own demons,*
*angry enough to surrender. Fill me,*
*O Spirit of God with your Gift to lead when*
*I may want to sit it out. Push me gently*
*to dare to dance a tune for our time.*

CHAPTER FOUR

# ...And, the Wisdom To Know
# the Difference.

## Humans, Hope, and Expectations Go Hand In Hand
## With Christ

While my four sisters, two brothers and I waited each Friday for the bus to transport us to our parish school of St. Thomas the Apostle on Detroit's east side near Miller and Van Dyke, our hearts hoped that dad would arrive in time with jelly cakes and doughnuts. Dad worked the midnight shift at the Budd Company as a crane operator, and, on "pay day" he'd stop to get us treats before we mounted the bus, and he went to his day job.

Humans, hope and expectation go hand in hand in Jesus Christ who is in our midst already while Advent reminds us that we await His second coming at the end of time.

Hope is a powerful virtue that drives us as we long and desire, look, and watch, and wait for One to instill calm beyond fear, peace more than war, Love over indifference, fertile and fruitful lands of spring beyond barren despair, doubt, even wintry depression, and the lion and the lamb eating together, free from destroying the weak and innocent with terror. Hope lives! Hope lives in us also. Securing serenity in troubling times a day a time.

Like Advent candles processing at Mass for insertion into the circular, global, evergreen wreath of high hope and expectation believers are aglow with the Light of love living, giving and causing us to forgive and stretch our views of things to match the Maker's all-encompassing heart.

When and where the hungry are fed, the homeless are sheltered, and the poor and rejected are borne up in charity, Jesus has come again (Mathew 24:37-44). The traditional and ever hopeful corporal and spiritual works of mercy radiate in Advent Catholics proclaim Vatican II's clarion call for "full, active, and conscious participation" at Mass and in our streets, schools, homes, and hearts the belief that "He will come again in glory to judge the living and the dead," of our creed.

The wisdom of Jesus Christ awaits being born in us this Advent and every day of our breathing and being about his ministry of healing hurting hearts, beating swords into plowshares and spears into pruning hooks, and innocent children playing safely over the adder's nest. In other words, as the Apostle James saw it, "Religion that is pure and undefiled is this: To care for orphans and widows in distress.' Such awe and Light.

Advent is about the Word made flesh who passionately longs for us these days of expectation and hope. God passionately loves us with a commitment to never leave us abandoned or orphaned. That passion promises Light amid darkness of political, social and individual tyrannies and despots overcome. God's passion lures us no less!

### New Year's Resolution No Time To Jest

One acquaintance says she'll be joining Curves next week as a new year's resolution for 2005. Another spoke of the Atkins and South Beach diets. Me? I'll resolve to live one day at a time, moment by moment relishing Father and Mother Time's fleeting face, numbering my weeks or months, my ebbing energy at each day's end.

Resolutions seem to fall out of fashion once they're readily engaged with all good intentions to follow through on them. I notice the rising crowds in the gyms early in January and, by mid-February, and sooner for some, physical fitness goes by the wayside. Along with other resolutions, I suppose.

Nevertheless, resolutions give pause to evaluate and reflect on life's virtue and value. Without them, life seems to steer in aimless, rampant ways. Addictions tend to replace all the merit in personal goals and objectives and one's wellbeing.

A long time ago, I recall someone telling me the story of the jester. The jester seemed to teach wisdom in her foolish ways. Once upon a time, the jester acted so foolish that the King gave her his walking stick with instructions to keep it until she found a bigger fool than herself.

As time unfolded, the King became critically ill. With his family and God's middlemen and ministers near his side, in a weakened state, the king voiced: "I am going on a journey from which I will not return, so, I called you here to bid you farewell."

The jester stepped forth upon hearing the King's farewell address.

"Your Majesty, when you crisscrossed the lands and kingdoms over the seas to meet with your people, your nobles and foreign powers, your servants always went before you, making necessary preparations. May I ask what preparations Your Majesty has made for this long journey before you now?"With his head bowed, as he lay in his bed, the King mumbled: Alas, I have made no plans."

Leaning over the King's bed, the jester handed the King the walking stick for she had found a bigger fool than herself.

Father and Mother Time alert the world's inhabitants and guests to live each day fully with preparation and planning for life to come, and responsible care and stewarding of the earth's resources.

Mortal men and women will die one day. That's something citizens of this land push off refusing to hear about the reality that one day each human's life ends. Period. The eternal quest for the 'ever young Puer and Puella', humans are not. None departs this globe alive. And, humans like to shout that heaven can wait, however. So do I. 2005 bids this land's dwellers to hear the wisdom of Scripture's psalmist who writes in the Good Book: "Without a vision, a people perish."

Christianity, among the worlds religions worthy of attention, reminds mortal beings of the inevitably of one's demise. Knowing that is freeing in that it helps humans focus on the truly important matters in life. Matters beyond this life's longings take center stage in New Time. After all, hearts are restless and looking for love in all the wrong places, all the sad faces, until they rest in the ultimate meaning maker, one ancient St. Augustine of Hippo, Africa similarly warned in the Christian calendar's first decade. Bring on the resolutions, and "let's roll" with Mother and Father Time.

## Springtime Settles In

Fresh Air! Love it, don't you? A nice cool breeze, not so cold. Brisk, slapping wind won't do. Hurry on, Spring!

Welcome to Lent that begins our 40-day jaunt in the middle of pain, a path in converting, and the promise of Easter. Call it the pilgrim's progress inching ever so slowing, falling and getting up. Resilient find resourceful.

The classic three ways or movements mount these Lenten (means springtime, from the Old English, "lencten") days. Teresa of Avila and John of the Cross, Joseph Campbell, (departure, initiation, and return) J.R. Tolkien (all Catholic, by the way), among others, depict the movement, the struggle for good over evil, and the race for the crown, the Meaning, Purpose in life.

Mel Gibson's last hours of Christ's life, the drama, and his birthing of this brutally violent crucifixion emerged from his own emerging from the emptiness of celebrity and soul. Relating his own addictive path, Mel Gibson needed the path of Purpose he lost (Mt. 5:1-12). His purgative (uncovering) and removal of the masks (addictions) had him crawling like an infant in his quest for God and meaning. He began to walk toward God's ever-loving embrace in his illuminata (discovery) of the Light shining on his achey-breaky heart. Finally, he runs into the arms of the Beloved in his unitiva (recovery) and divine union with the Divine Psychotherapist.

The path and promise entails pain, rejection, hurt, disappointment, betrayal and the dark night of the soul. Spring has its revenge on winter. Out of death stems Christ's blooming fragrance of the wonderful Wind of a welcome Breeze. An aroma of Life lingers everywhere. Lilies and tulips poke up from down under. Then comes the Morning. Finally. Fully. Fruitfully. Lovely Light. First, the cross. The Crown. Welcome Easter.

## The Cry of "Macho" Men

"If you have searched for a men's group to bond and discuss men's issues, then you will want to meet in the parish meeting room Monday at 8P.M." That promotional piece in the church bulletin prompted a dozen men to gather and "birth" a men's group that met around myth and the masculine, story, struggles and joys. Little did the group know that they were realizing what psychologist and mentor Sam Keen said in his best selling book bought by both women and men, *Fire in the Belly*: "Friendship may be the best antidote for the alienation that is the inevitable result of corporate and professional styles of life."

When the group convened, they were encouraged to stay with the weekly meeting of a couple hours for at least five sessions before opting out. Most honored that request and continue to meet in the same group or as members of another men's group.

Joseph Campbell's story from Arabian Nights marked my memory that first meeting with the importance of men's meetings, bonding and beholding the mystery and misery of each member's sacred story. Imagination and myth is key to Campbell's story of the man who is plowing his field, when suddenly his plow is stopped and stuck. The man digs deep down and there he finds an iron ring. As he pulls up on the ring, he discovers that it's a cave filled with jewels. Like many stories, Campbell asserts that," Where you stumble, there your treasure is."

For me it was as though I stumbled into the group out of my painful need to connect with the energy of brothers that I hadn't felt since the time a small group of four of us met while I was an inner city pastor in Detroit. Memories of those very early morning meetings emerged with the wonderment of why I waited so long to bond once more.

Could it have been Campbell's story that stirred something within me about how failure and stumbling doesn't get positive press in today's culture? Or, rather, was it my inability to dig deep as the man in the story who was stuck? Was I unwilling to look into the recesses of my own shadow as religious psychologist Karl Jung suggests, and bring that dark underground to light, to consciousness? Could I have been stuck too long, unlike the man who digs deep when his plow is paralyzed? Could my numbness to imagine what could be in my deepest desires and dreams been realized long before stumbling into this men's group that changed my life?

My experience became one in which I would make mistakes, fail and fall, but get right back up, brush off the dust and band-aid the bruises while watching so that nobody saw me fall. Dig deeper when I stumbled, not me! I wouldn't even allow for tears. Tears weren't manly, I protested. So, I got up and kept right on going. I wasn't much into shovels and shadows and stopping in my "stuckness" to reach deep within and pay attention to the pain and misery and mystery of being a man in need of mending.

My new group saved me from myself. The group and energy I found that helped me to dig as the members provided a safe place to explore belonging, ownership, inclusion, influence, tenderness and intimacy in a way that I would not allow before I stumbled into the men's group. Now, I play, drum, and tell stories and laugh.

I confessed that my culture wanted me to be a perfect man. I wanted to be the successful and "perfect" priest. Consequently, I avoided any semblance of stumbling, or looking bad. Thus I remained stuck. I would not dig. I played the role of priest for a long time. I think I even became my role as I refused to admit failure.

So now, by the Grace of God, go I! I plow, get stuck, fail and fall, get up, dig deep and behold the treasure. The Men's group helped do that. I'm glad I stumbled into that group.

## End Teen Violence with Fatherly Advice

Summer has given way to September and the sound of school bells ringing. Will gunfire ring out in schoolyards again, too? No, we hope and pray. No more balloons and bows of green, yellow, red, and blue to mark the sites of shootings by school bullies.

Mind you, it isn't little girls who are doing the shooting.

Mothers and women apparently tend to do a better job of bonding with girls. They admit pain more readily. Males on the other hand, have trouble expressing weakness and admitting feelings. And this, I believe, predisposes men to be quick to shoot with deadly guns.

Some so-called experts conclude that these schoolyard-shooter boys are exceptional. Some say they are aberrations. A few shout about poor parenting and a lack of supervision.

Could this new trend in schools be an ontological issue – a quest for meaning? Purpose? Perhaps. But I think much, much more is going on here.

Rev. Richard Rohr, a Franciscan priest and leader of retreats throughout the world, has studied various cultures to see how each turns boys into men. Rohr's findings make the most sense to me for a solution to the schoolyard violence criss-crossing our nation.

In his research, Rohr discovered that culture after culture felt that if a young man between 13 and 16 was not introduced to the mysteries or pains of life, then the young man would not know how to handle pain, loss, alienation, and rejection.

There is pain in many of the realities young men experience in the world. You are not the center of the universe; life is hard; you win some and lose some; one day you will die; you are not in control; your life is about something or Some one bigger than you. If a young man can't deal with his pain, Rohr concludes, he abuses his power.

However, "for the man who has descended into the drowning waters and come upon the other side, for the initiate who has been in the belly of the whale and spit up on the shore, there is an ultimate new shape to the universe," Rohr wrote in *Sojourner Magazine*.

When it comes to the violence enveloping this nation's youth, are we reaping what we sow? Can we do things differently with boys; things that demand a shift in the way boys are introduced and initiated into reality?

What seems to be needed is a time of initiation; a weekend where fathers, sons, and grandfathers can check into a local hotel or hike into a pastoral woods together; a time when young males can hear about the realities of life's struggles, limitations, pain, death, and difficulties.

Of course, that will take some doing in a culture fascinated with fast food, instant potatoes, and quick fixes. This ritual bonding of fathers and sons will require well spent – sons staring in the faces of their own fathers; sons being equipped by the experiences of their fathers with the armor needed to confront life's predicaments.

Guns and gangs don't have to win. Fathers can mend the male soul. America will move in the right direction when it stops to pause and ponder the worth of each son and begins to tell each one the terrible truths about growing up.

## How to Deal with Crisis?

Seven ways may be helpful for individuals, families, churches and organizations to face into the crisis of violence in a constructive and helpful manner:

1. *Purpose* — Unless the individual, family or institution has a defined reason or goal in mind (and heart), it becomes easy to lose focus, miss the aim, and be distracted in numerous ways. Perhaps, the family budget is a good example. How individuals or groups spend their money is a good indicator of the purpose people espouse. If little or no money is set aside for the needy of the neighborhood or world, the purpose can get fogged up by spending all the money on self or family. This ignores the Gospel purpose at hand to share and be good stewards of the gifts and resources God gave us for the common sourcing of all.

   One's work or need to make a lot of money can also cause blur of focus; and, in fact, do violence to the family who may be given very little quality time and caring with a parent or other family or group members. Forgetting self and aiming for the good of the family or group may well set the purpose sailing to success

   Monitoring the television and what one watches can help prevent harmful, destructive, or violent ways from easily finding their way into the family living room. We would never allow a thief or bad influence into our home; so, why allow anything to gain entry in the home by way of television? Other questions to keep asking daily at supper may be: Why are we here on earth? Why did God make us? Are we really heading toward heaven by the way we live each day? Am I a loving person? Do I care about others? When did I see Jesus recently or today at work, school, on the playground? What is my own or the family's project for the week? Is the project related essentially to Christ? What would Christ have us do? What would Jesus do?

2. *Pride* — Feeling good about who I am within a family or group is essential to working on the purpose of project. Helping children to settle conflict by sending them to their rooms until they work out an interpersonal conflict may well enable them to be on the way to peacemaking. That is, if mom or dad, or older sister or brother, or even the baby-sitter, is willing to monitor the negotiations after they emerge from the room. Discussion of what they decided is important. Helping children to feel good about how they determined their plan of action as to resolving their own conflict will enable a healthy sense of pride.

3. *Prayer* — Conversations with the Lord are important to settling differences. Youngsters as well as older persons need to witness each other praying for guidance when turmoil embroils in the home, workplace, school or nation. Asking each person in the room or around the table to say something to God is a most valuable lesson to be learned, especially by the children. Confidence and pride is built by taking little steps. Questions to ask include: Do I really pray? Are my prayer, worship and attendance at Mass really making a difference? Does my prayer provide a context to deal with life? Do I have a regularly scheduled time for prayer? Does my prayer include intentions for my enemy?

4. *Persistence* — Like the widow of the Gospel who keeps at Jesus, do I keep at my project, purpose, plan for the

day or week? Moving back to the purpose is important. In fact, having the purpose written out on a beautiful large poster board or banner can readily help all to persist in accomplishing the purpose. Do I grow weary when I find the purpose difficult to act upon? Am I a team player with the purpose, or do I only enact those parts that I like?

5. **Peacemaking** — A regular time when persons or families can reflect on forgiveness helps rid violence from the heart. Just before or after a meal is an ideal time to help one another confront indecency in my own life and to ask

6. **Forgiveness** of others for disregarding their dignity as a person made in God's own image and likeness. Do I try to be a peace-maker? Am I willing to go to another person seeking forgiveness or do I always expect others to come to me?

7. *Patience* — Easy docs it. Trying to push the purpose to the extremes may be possible for adults but a grave injustice for children. Expecting solutions to happen overnight is unrealistic and damaging to the relationships formed in setting the purpose, project or plan in the first place. Patience is a virtue. Seeing results may not be possible in one's own time, but the fruits of such labor may be celebrated by those who come after us. We didn't get to this violent way of life overnight; nor, will we be more caring immediately. Ask God for patience. Am I good to myself or do I expect too much to happen too fast? Am I in line with Gospel patience; or, have I bought into the culture's need for instant gratification and instant solutions now?

8. *Perspective* — Balance is necessary when striving to help free society of violence. Forcing my ways onto another is not only a violation of another's person, but an approach that people are apt to flee from rather than embrace. Trying to do too much may also be harmful. Crusading for self rather than for Christ's peace and non-violence is off the mark also. Time for leisure, play and

silence is beneficial and necessary to carrying out the purpose. Can I be still? Is genuine leisure a reality in my life? Do I gain my perspective from the Scriptures? Do I take time for family, friends, and co-workers? Do I seek counsel with one or more persons with whom I share my joys, hopes, frustrations, and disappointments? What in me is a blessing to others? What is damaging to me and my neighbor or children? Do I really know myself? How? What are my peak moments, life story, and family of origin? Are others better for my presence? Are others more joy-filled because of my peace?

## Summary

Peace, non-violence, human decency and love won't be in short supply if caring and compassion are what distribute it. Our generous and abundant God gives plenty of love for all. It can become; however, like so many other things, a question of distribution. Am I holding onto or keeping God's love for myself alone?

Purpose, pride, prayer, persistence, peacemaking, patience and perspective must be clearly defined and owned by the individual, family, group, institution, or nation if human indecency is to be rooted out and replaced by care and compassion for all. Good old fashioned virtues and practices may well add to peace in our time. The metaphor of one on his or her knees in prayer is an act of surrender to God's will and way. It suggests an open posture of faith in a God who reaches out to embrace humanity in stewarding well the earth. Courage to make a difference is fear that has said its prayers daily.

A Chinese proverb sums up ways to peace and serenity in troubling times:
:

> *"If there is righteousness in the heart,*
> *there will be beauty in the character.*
> *If there is beauty in the character,*
> *there will be love in the home.*

*If there is love in the home,*
*there will be order in the nation.*
*If there is order in the nation,*
*there will be peace in the world."*

## What The Nun Study Teaches!

What the Nun Study Teaches Us!

*Aging with Grace: What the Nun Study Teaches Us About Leading Longer Healthier, and More Meaningful Lives.*

Visits with my mother's oldest sister, Gertie had me puzzled about her own 25-year bout with her killer along with 4 million other Americans afflicted with Alzheimer's disease. More staggering are predictions that by the year 2050 that number will swell to 14 million.

Little did I understand that fateful brain disease that had my aunt staring and pointing to the ceiling as if longing to reach the heavens. But now with the honorable and reverential aid of 678 School Sisters of Notre Dame, dubbed as the Nun Study, I am able to understand much more. Thanks to Aging With Grace, the story of an altar boy who dreamed of being a gymnast and a farmer, whose calling is an epidemiologist researcher, has Dr. David Snowden, a graduate of the University of Minnesota beginning his study the same year in 1986.

A tale and journey in twelve chapters twists and turns down convent corridors to table where Snowden joined the sisters in playing cards and ending up faithful friends.

For example, 106-year-old Sister Esther Boor, the longest living School Sister of Notre Dame, is one of five Nun Study participants who lapped 3 centuries and still engages exercise on her stationery bicycle and ceramics – living testimony of a life of grace offering a prescription of keeping active to maintain mental, spiritual and physical well-being even in extreme old age.

Then there's Sister Nicolette Welter, 93-years old and the lone surviving member of her class who took vows more than 7 decades ago. With 2 of her siblings, also School Sisters of Notre Dame, Sister Claverine (86) and Sister Ursula (92), their mental aliveness and longevity is in their prescription of walking a few miles daily. Their own early formation must have emphasized the power of exercise, coupled with daily praying and meditation because I witnessed the same healthy prescription for good health in two School Sisters of Notre Dame, Sister Elizabeth and Sister Mary, who "charged" the circling grounds often on the campus of Scared Heart School of Theology in Milwaukee where we were colleagues in spiritual and human development for older men aspiring to be priests.

Snowden's startling statistical correlation between expressing positive emotions and longevity is illustrated in the study as Dr. Snowden writes: "Aging is not the cause of the health problems of old age, disease is the culprit."

Upon death, the good sisters even gave their brains for lifestyle, genetic, diet, education and personality assessments, coupled with the number of dental fillings a sister has – all of which has concluded the menu for a longer, healthier, and happier life.

Among findings:

Why linguistic ability early in one's childhood development seems to protect against Alzheimer's. That has Dr. Snowden prescribing for parents to read often to their children.

Which foods, like stewed tomatoes and pink grapefruit, along with the role of folic acid seem to preserve healthy brains. The importance of meals together and how one's heart, mind, and soul get nourished with one's body. Why stroke prevention with exercise and diet may be key to staving off Alzheimer's symptoms.

How moderate healthy lifestyle and education, coupled with meaning and purpose in one's life, spirituality, faith and a support system help in the aging process. In fact, Snowden reports that the risk of death in any given year after age 65 is about 25 percent less for School Sisters of Notre Dame than it is for the general population of women in the United States.

Why preventing or treating depression is crucial to healthy aging. Snowden found a link between chronic depression and Alzheimer's, while the Nun Study showed that emotions expressed in autobiographies scripted when the sisters were in their early twenties could project longevity sixty or seventy years later.

Saturated with told secrets and successes of venerable sisters in aging well, Aging With Grace inspires, informs and fills one soul with what early spiritual mentors, monks, and sages knew all along: A time of true grace through old age is possible and the promise of the "abundant life" that the Scriptures prescribes long before this notable scientific study, validates the wisdom passed on to those willing to embrace.

It is only now, however, that baby boomers, among other Americans, may be ready to tread a healthier path than one reeled with consumption, anxiety and freneticism without grace.

An "easy" read, it had this page-turner cozy up in my easy chair relishing uncommon pearls and nuggets of grace, like a sponge soaking up the sage advice of women too often unheard. A "down home" journey of untold magnitude, grateful hearts will savor the long-standing aroma of the School Sisters of Notre Dame, among so may sisters today in America who do a world of good. With Snowden I heard myself saying: Amen! So be it!

### Anger Reminders for Raging Times

Use these thoughts before anger or rage flare. Keep them near to remind you of what you already know but may forget when angry.

Remember that anger lurks when you think you're being treated unjustly.

Feelings like mad, sad, glad, or scared help you cope.

No one can make you angry. Walk away from your anger daily.

You choose or decide to be angry or enraged.

Step aside and take a deep breath when anger looms.

Tell the person you're experiencing anger with that you need to cool off and decide on a time to meet later.

Storing angry feelings within yourself will cause havoc on your body.

Express your anger in appropriate, non-violent ways.

Remember that conflict is normal; *violence* **is** *not.*

Getting enraged doesn't help anyone, most of all, yourself.

When angry, *name* the problem making you upset; *claim* the issue as your own.

Then, you can *tame* the way you handle the problem.

Own your angry feelings.

When younger, if a girl, you may have been told to stuff your anger. "Boys won't like girls who get angry," you may have been told. *Unlearn that.*

If you're a boy, you may have been told that men don't cry. *Unlearn that.*

It's how you express the feelings that will endanger others.

Remember that everyone is incomplete and capable of falling short of ideals.

Try to put yourself into other's shoes.

Remember to get help if your anger is out of control.

Unresolved anger could become resentment and cynicism.

Ask God to help you let go of angry feelings.

In the Sermon on the Mount, Jesus says, "You shall not kill," and adds to it the proscription of anger, hatred, and vengeance. Mat.5:21.

*Wisdom:*
*Live in me discerning sage. Move me*
*beyond logic and analysis to wise ways within.*
*tried and tested Truth tickle my complacency*
*with your ways yet untried! Amen*

CHAPTER FIVE

# Living One Day at a Time

## My Tale of Three Decades Told

*You were their rock,*
*their fortress, and their might;*
*You, Lord, their Captain*
*in the well-fought fight;*
*You in the darkness drear,*
*their one true light.*

Three decades after voicing, "I will, with the help of God," my resolve to serve as a servant of God stands unshaken, thanks be to the Creator who makes all things possible. Any married person vowed to love knows a path of sacrifice better than me, for sure. Yet, I follow forth a path of mystery and intrigue and wonder unsure where it leads. Questions I will always have, speaking up, I refuse to sit, standing sure this much I know in faith. And, this is enough for this human inching on behind God.

From early on, an attraction for being a priest powerfully pulled me. And, despite a clerical culture of denial, silence and shame at times, I am more convinced than ever that the People of God know that church comprises all. The path and procession seeking the Holy Face is a pilgrimage of pauper and pope, peasant and president in route to a tent beyond this earthly one that St. Paul addresses.

A priest's tale is one of love. It involves doing the right thing, standing up like the late Fathers William Cunningham of Focus Hope, or Corktown's Clement Kern, the conscience of Detroit, when others choose to sit down, to be silent, and to defer. A tale like that of Thomas Gumbleton, shepherdly bishop, is the story of priestly life. It is one of letting the Pharaoh go, like a Puah and Shiprah in Exodus, mid-wifing life, letting the Pharaoh go do his destructive thing, and servant of God free to follow God's truth in love.

When one speaks up, one will be ostracized and judged disloyal or, even worse, "breaking communion." Prophets paved that way, however. For them it became easier to be shunned for a greater Good and God gripped their hearts.

What is clear to me is that this last half-century watched the largest exodus from the priesthood since the Reformation, a vocation I love and have spoken to others about pursuing. While it is a tale of paradox, all of life is like that: When weak I am strong, lose your life to find it, you win some and lose some. God is there in this tale. Always. All ways.

Despite a clerical culture, heartaches by the number, and obstruction to gathering all for conversation around God's Table to resolve problems plaguing church and society, sociologist Father Andrew Greeley's research has me concurring with his summary:

"In the short run I anticipate a reaction to 2004 like that to the birth-control encyclical - a decline in church attendance and a decline in financial contributions but no mass exodus from Catholicism. Catholics, even very angry Catholics, still like being Catholic." (Priests: A Calling in Crisis) Evergreen hope here in this tale.

Sure, it's the signs and symbols, sacraments and incense, stained glass windows, Tables of Word and Holy Communion, good times and bad, sickness and health, and, an older, graying assembly of Catholics with a median age of priests at 60. But, it's more. It's the discipline and routine of spiritual and corporal works of mercy justly mending a global pie where some few countries selfishly grab more than their share. It's the enthusiasm one is saturated with to go out and teach all nations this Love.

It's beauty and beast, weed and wheat, agony and ecstasy,

consolation and desolation, mystery and misery all merging mightily in song:

> For all the saints,
> who from their labor rest,
> All who their faith
> before the world confessed,
> Your name, O Jesus,
> be forever blest!

My tale of three decades, ordained in 1976, challenges my clerical culture of silence and denial to build bridges of trust and affection, care of soul, and mending many, especially the least among us that no one else may want. To ignite each one's dignity and worth, awakening it in self and others, states my mission in Christ.

With Hebrews of the Sacred Scriptures, chapter 5, I am confident that "every priest has been taken out of humankind and is appointed to act for others in their relations to God, to offer gifts and sacrifices for sins; and so he can sympathize with those who are ignorant or uncertain because he too lives in the limitations of weakness (Hebrews 5:1-2).

Armed with love, then, and Communion cup and chalice of copper, like an earthen vessel hammered with the hurts of life's path, broken, even bruised, it is the copper's ability to be (re)formed again and again in abuses of life. With the cup of Life and Communion of sacrifice and shield of God's Word, all will be well; all matter of things will be well. If not now, one day, thanks be to God who leads the parade anyhow, even though I may think some days I am General Manager and Operating Officer of the universe.

With seventy-five millions Catholics in the USA, I plow ahead with urgency and confidence that God is smack in the middle of life's messes: "No one who sets a hand to the plow and looks to what was left behind is fit for the kingdom of God" (Lk 9:62).

Trappist monk Thomas Merton, in The School of Charity Letters, writes:

"We are asleep, and our prayers are little more than trances. We are inarticulate, we are deaf-mutes: and only you, who have been silenced by a vow, really have your tongues loosed, and can speak, because you are not concerned with arguments and justifications before men, but only with speaking to God and His angels and His saints."

Once more, with the Catholic sign of the Cross, I begin and end with AMEN!, as I relish and savor baptism as a believer 55 years later. So be it!

## Red Run River's Ducks and Fish

Nearing the end of my 4-mile, early morning walk and jog on Maple Road, just north of Fourteen Mile Road in Sterling Heights, Michigan, where I live, I pause on the bridge over Red Run River. I look over the railing, leaning on my arms. I watch as the bright sun glares on the waves of the sandy-colored water below me. It is refreshing, let alone relaxing to relish and savor the moment, brief though it be. Nature has a hold on me.

When still enough to notice, I am awestruck by ducks in V-formation surrounding three young ones. The ducks are somewhat frightened by the intruder overhead, peering down on them. They seem to grow comfortable with me. Westbound they continue with little effort, it seems. Their webbed-feet hold them upon the water's top. Their heads, with eyes on either side, observe their surroundings, perhaps for danger or predators or even humans who may harm their swim this sunny Saturday morning.

Beneath these beautiful creations swim long fish. At first I didn't notice them. What are they? I cannot name them. Their wiggle, however, caught my attention. They hovered under the ducks almost suspecting them to be food. Quickly, they move on, after assessing the ducks. The fish also seem to have a formation as they glide in the water of Red Run, though their swim is less predictable than the ducks I set my eyes upon.

Like ourselves, I thought, the formations of ducks and fish, and the boundaries and parameters of human beings, seem to be necessary for life. Children, like the ducklings surrounded by mother and father duck, need a playpen, if you will, of safety, of lines not to be crossed by others or themselves. Similar to the creation account in the Bible's Book of Genesis, Adam and Eve, representatives of humankind, are told by God to enjoy the garden. They are to observe boundaries, however, not to cross. They disobey. The common good is compromised. Self absorbed and selfish wants wreak havoc on humans, on self, on nature.

Tempted by demonic forces, like ourselves, they are told they would become God if they ate of the forbidden tree in the garden. They cross boundaries. They sin, in fact.

Whether it's the world champion Detroit Pistons bound by the parameters of the floor on which the ball is dribbled, or the Detroit Tigers in Comerica Park, or the Red Wings in their hockey town confines of the ice, we all have to "play" the game of life respecting boundaries and sacred space of others that we dare not enter. After all, all abuse of power is about ignoring boundaries or civil or human rights of citizens, and the most vulnerable among us. When youngsters are sexually abused, boundaries are violated by adults who should know better. Impaired, however by illness, ignorance or foolishness, inappropriately children are shamed when an adult abuses power and them.

God's order of creation has a rhythm and pattern of its own. Like the ebb and flow of ducks and fish and us, we all need to pause, take notice, and appreciate with respect boundaries enjoyed by all of creation. We're all better for boundaries, even blessed.

### Tale of Love, Marriage and More

Love and marriage go together like . . .

In the headlines today we read: Attacks in 5 Iraqi Cities Leave More Than 100 Dead. Tears well up within me.

Choices of love, of marriage like Joni and Don joining hearts this Saturday in Melvindale, Michigan. Other choices, others make this day, less than love, however.

Joni and Don choose to dwell in the kingdom of God. Their choice requires sacrifice. Personal sacrifice. Like prophets of old, you choose this day to make a difference in our world, right where you live and reside and work. Congratulations! Swimming upstream is no easy task in a world where death and destruction and an "easy come, easy go" culture throws away anything I don't like or want or feel good about. Don't go there! Even in the belly of the whale, Jonah emerged from the dark into Light!

Like Moses and his reluctance and wrestling with God to lead the people to the Promised Land, your time together in committed and lifelong Matrimony will find you questioning, even tempted perhaps to graze greener grounds. That's human. But, don't go there. Ever. Be for each other and our world the choice you make before us and the world today.

Live in love. There is no better choice than to love.

"I will be with you," God assures the worrying Moses, and perhaps you and me. God invites lovers. No force here. Only the power of persuasion. With God's "I will be with you. No one who sets a hand to the plow and looks to what was left behind is fit for the Kingdom of God" (Luke 9:62).

Your vows today, coupled with the Word of God and our Holy Communion with you assures you that there will be suffering and sacrifice, aches and pain, the beauty and the beast, the agony and the ecstasy, the consolation and desolations of resting in each other's arms.

Your love today, enveloped in good times and bad, in sickness and in health, is not TV's Search for Tomorrow, the Days of Our Lives, and As the World Turns or the Young and the Restless. You choose today what comes your way. You commit. You choose to love. And, tears flow that Love lives. Still. Love lives. In you, in each other!

Know that God is with you! Stay the course. Plow the field where you live, not looking back. Live in God's dwelling. Love.

Love and marriage go together like . . .

**So True of Sterling Heights: Fresh, Friendly, and Familiar**

What is it that would have Sterling Heights, Michigan named among the best cities to raise children? As I recall, that accolade was pinned on this town some time ago. Undoubtedly it is the people, its parks, and the way it is managed that makes it such a pleasure to reside here.

Sterling Heights' planners envisioned the park, nature center, and library off Dodge Park and Utica roads. All are child-friendly and safe places for our kids. People project an upbeat attitude in all of these sites, and at Freedom Hill, buzzing with popular concerts and festivals and fun-filled activities for all. The voluminous library on Dodge Park is outstanding also and child-friendly.

Furthermore, if one simply wishes to stroll and job along Schoenherr from 14 Mile road north, fear for one's well-being is farthest from this runner's mind. Even Wolfgang, this writer's Bichon Frise dog, delights in his daily walks through this friendly city. All inhabitants here seem to relish in the crisp, cool surroundings of fall tree coloring, character and charm for Sterling Heights. Although I have yet to visit the Senior Center on Utica Road, my bet is that our wise elders who frequent there would echo similar sentiments about Sterling Heights.

While the people, its parks and centers provide the pleasure, one has to include the impact our places of worship has on teens, for example, not to mention the many others who make God a central place in their homes and hearts. For example, across denominational lines, a recent survey from the University of Michigan showed that high school senior demonstrated less scrapes with the law and with drugs and drink when they worshipped weekly.

The same high school seniors, the survey found, were more inclined to exercise and engage in civic affairs. Sterling Heights' many worship sites can take pride in their influence on believers. Good, effective pastors led this town's worship communities. St. Malachy Church, for example, Father Joseph Gembala leads an assembly of a few thousand households. A former civil attorney and perennial University of Michigan football fan takes time for kin and enjoyment at his alma mater's games, Father Joe is also faithfully found working nearby Warren's Cousino High School football games supporting his parishioner players. Furthermore, his heart is so convinced of youth ministry that minister Henrietta Steiner and countless teens (Casey, Kevin, Shawn, Brian, Pam, Chrissy to name a few also work part-time in the St. Malachy Parish Center answering phones and serving parishioners). Volunteers turned the front part of a barely-used house into a youth center a year ago. Catholic

social teaching is lived in the reach of teens of St. Malachy Church
in many ways. These bright, articulate Church leaders, like their
pastor, will be a mainstay of the virtues they practice for years to
come. His engaging and informed conversations add joy to my days.

A relatively new ministry of parish nurse at St. Malachy's has
Debra Christensen providing blood pressure readings, and a host of
other wellbeing opportunities for body, soul, and spirit. Helping
survivors in their grief at the death of a loved one or visits to the
Alzheimer's Home on 14 Mile is pastoral minister and Immaculate
Heart of Mary Sister Alys Curvier, IHM. Numerous parishioners
take seriously the second Vatican Council ('62-65) teaching that the
people are the Church (*Dogmatic Constitution on the Church*).
Their own witness value to the Gospel at home, school, in the
neighborhood or at work also enhances the life of Sterling Heights.
The 40-year old Vatican Council wrapped dignity around countless
numbers of Catholics who learned to enlarge "pray, pay, and obey."
They love their church and deserve applause for carrying it so
lovingly and so well.

At neighboring St. Rene Goupil Parish on Ryan, north of 15
Mile Road, where the late Monsignor F. Gerald Martin was founding pastor in 1970, the leadership of the people was obvious in my
effort to stay out of their way and let them bloom when I served as
associate pastor there from 1979-1982. Concurrently, I was director
of the ecumenical Michigan Coalition for Human Rights. Martin's
own love of the poor was supported by the Parish's St. Vincent
DePaul Society and Catholic social teaching that he was fond of
quoting in further forming his enthusiastic and Vatican II-shaped
parish family. Parish staffer Shirley Sills serves singles and elders
of this parish where we worked together.

While other Sterling Heights parishes of St. Jane Frances de
Chantel, St. Blasé, and St. Ephrem cluster in education and forma-
tion events, each has its own unique personality and clearly adds to
the vibrancy of this town. St. Matthias, St. Michael, SS. Cyril and
Methodius, and Our Lady of Czestohowa churches are situated in
Sterling Heights also.

Sister Joyce Campbell, an Immaculate Heart of Mary sister
serves in campus ministry at neighboring Warren's Macomb

Community College, where she has given her life to the development of young people for over three decades. While at St. Rene Parish, I also enjoyed leading liturgy for college students there as chaplain. The "unsung" efforts of so many Catholic nuns, priests, deacons, and faithful continue to leave their positive mark on many. We are better for them. This fresh, friendly, and familiar town works at shaping lives and forming community from the youngest to our senior citizens. It shows! Services provided enhance the wellbeing of this pleasurable city. Prompt police attention to problems and other city workers' dedication also help to enhance the esteem, dignity, and worth of each resident.

Although I miss the Arcola Street neighborhood of Detroit where neighbors were more united when I was growing up, this young town and its baby-boomers came full circle back to faith after letting it go in their quest for the "good life." Everyone plays his or her part in keeping this place clean and lively. Those values were handed on from our own parents whose faith and fervor never floundered. We are all better for the beliefs of all the religious assemblies here. Faith dashes fears with fresh new Light for peace in the coming holy days of Christmas and Hanukah. The Garfield campus of Macomb Community College will tease and tempt with holiday specials. Judy Collins thrilled this theatre-goer with her Christmas show there a few years ago. Michael Bolton at Freedom Hill this summer could be heard from my home across from the family-friendly Roger's Roost on Schoenherr, north of 14 Mile Road. Outstanding entertainers come to town often.

It is a privilege to share in the joys, hopes and struggles of family life all about me as a priest who knows of the respect this town has for its spiritual leaders. All of its hands help to shape a genuine town for raising children, our most important citizens, and all others, especially the wise elders who pass on virtues, customs, practices, and rites that made the soul of this city so rich. So much good speaks to one's pleasure in calling Sterling Heights, "My town!"

**Failure**

It has a lot to do with direction, guiding, and leading people well. A pastor once remarked, "Sometimes mud in the face is what helps people learn." Making mistakes and growing from them brings a leader forward. Sometimes I think that until one reaches 40, one is unteachable. At 40 one is finally ready for failure.

The child who isn't permitted to fall will never walk tall. If a child isn't free to rise from a fallen state, a golden opportunity is missed. The parent is to free the teenager to learn to walk well. Not only that, however, a nourishing parent enables the adolescent to walk away from home. All of the complexities of parental, religious and civic leadership. Gentle persuasion frees people to walk confidently in the face of forces that may knock one down. Rising beyond failure, shortcomings, mistakes, and even one's self assists in showing the way that is better than yesterday or today.

Failure can freeze and paralyze people forever. It doesn't have to, however. Mistakes can free. Failure has to be tempered by openness to get on with life in the midst of mistakes. Accepting failure affords one the inevitable opportunity to make progress.

**Thanksgiving Day: An Attitude of Gratitude Is a Pure Prayer**

Thanksgiving Day: It stops me in my tracks. It slows me right down. Ruffles my feathers, you may say. Thanksgiving opens my heart, hands, and mind. It tugs at my heartstrings for truths learned in life a half century:

I notice more. I know that life is short. So I savor it. Pause, Relax. Pursue, satisfying and meaningful moments.

Try to illumine the dark, dreary days of November. Tell a story, or a. joke. Love lady silence and solitude. Tolerate losses and let them go. Sing. Smile more widely. Whistle. Dance. Be fearless and stand up for someone or something when everyone else is sitting down. Tackle terror's challenges. Don't panic.

Be honest. Be all I can be. Laugh deeply. Overlook a lot. Lighten up. Love anyway.

Let the rat race by. Praise the Creator! Read something every day. Pack lightly. Honor your roots and relationships, even when they "bug" you. Balance your boat:, and your life. Lead. Heal. Do a good deed. Blow a bubble. Trust deepest dreams. Follow your heart's beat. Be a drum major for God's sake! Go up or down the stream and learn to breathe under water the whole life through.

Don't die before your time. Care for those no one else wants. Get a grip, not too tight though. Break bread. Do the turkey trot! Make fresh footprints in the snow. Shoot for the moon, or land among the stars. Glow! Watch that turkey crossing the road. Get a life. Pass the potatoes or the yams. Think of someone who was here last Thanksgiving Day. Have an attitude of gratitude – a pure prayer.

## Fallish Feeling Fades to Wonderland of White

Feeling Fallish. Fueled by November's thick air, rushing rain and down days. A mood of darks, grays, golden-brown-hued leaves gliding groundward with wind spins hurling them, coupled with my wonderment about all this change. Dancing leaves, flip-flopping in midair soar my spirit, dash my doubts and delight me mostly.

Overcast clouds cloud my eyes and weigh down my heart in a season of melancholy and Saturn, the Roman god of the wise and old elders who know better 'bout life's turns. My soul is saturated in it all. I like it all. Bare naked, skeletal trees tell tales that the truth is uncluttered, like an un-leaved tree's branches tossing, bending unbreakable, flexible this way and that. The feel of crisp cornstalks drying and dying stops me in my tracks.

Through it all, slight sunlight peeks, pokes effortful through shadowy-clouded masses and heavy-hearted moods marked by this time's wrestling, even wrenching challenges in its questions of one's soul. Crunchy and colored leaves tumbling up the sidewalk as if leading the way into one's deepest center, let alone around the block. And, more – pointing me inward.

Fall seems to close its door, giving way to winter's wonderland. The harvest of souls and fields finalized. Pumpkins picked, squash smashed in apple-sauce like fashion sprinkled with cinnamon aroma and the fragrance filling hearts and homes. The olfactory never gets enough of the penetrating, saturating, stuffing including Cornish hens and gobbling turkeys.

Feeling fallish. Its intrusion, invasion wakes me to much more. Season changes and the melancholy moods swell my heart with thanks in its fleeting moments of grandeur, gold, and grace. Gratefully, this human's harvest hails winter's harsh ice and biting cold balanced with soft, gentle snowflakes whitening another kind of unfolding beauty all about, like light overcoming every fallish feeling and darkened mood.

Welcome winter. Farewell fall.

## Love Your Neighbor as Yourself

"Love your neighbor as yourself." It amazes me how often that great commandment is misunderstood. The commandment seems to have its focus on one's neighbor more so than on one's self.

A lady recently told me of how little love she has for herself while at the same time, she mentioned how concerned and caring she is about others. It appears contradictory to think that we can love others while failing to love self first.

I remember a high school teacher once saying to me: "Love others first, ourselves last, and God at all times." Bewildered by that statement, I simply let it be — sure that it was asking the impossible. The wisdom of this great commandment rests in the fact that God requires us to love others only and in as much as we love self – no more, no less! The problem, however, is to learn how to wisely, gently, and adequately love self.

How can one love his or her neighbor and all the differences that one has when his or her love for self is not present within? At our ideal "best" people are lovers. Unlike the animal world, people are the only beings who have the ability to love; but, shortly after children are sent to school that capacity to love and appreciate that quality of love is diminished or entirely covered over and forgotten. When this talent to love is undeveloped, misinterpreted or blocked, we are in trouble. The worst in people comes first.

It is when our relationships with others are appreciated most that we experience the God who is love as the scriptures tell us. Couples only begin to speak of love of God after they have experienced their married love; and, they can only love each other after they have accepted themselves as loved.

A baby can only feel the love of a parent by the way in which he or she is held. To that extent will the child be able to understand the world as a friendly or hostile place. Consequently he or she will be able to love "neighbor" to the degree that love is felt in his or her own life. If we are to develop better relationships with people, regardless of race, color or creed, then the need to form a healthier love of self has to happen before we can reach out to our neighbors.

*O God Grant me*
*a brave and bold heart with*
*hands and feet to fill the environment*
*with Your aroma and fragrance of*
*calm, serenity and peace.*

# CHAPTER SIX

# Accepting Hardships As the Pathway to Peace

## A Time of Thanksgiving for Two Blessed Pioneers

My parents grew up in times and places when they experienced poverty and depression. They lived simple lives.

Although deceased, I cherish their sound values. I learned persistence and perseverance from their care and commitment for education.

Never did they send us to church while they stayed at home. They expected of us what they expected of themselves.

Obligation for the common good was obvious in civic responsibilities. Punctuality at work, even when they were keeping two jobs each, taught me the value of time.

They taught their family to save and spend wisely. At sixteen, they left northern Michigan homes for Detroit's factories, where their earnings were sent home to support large families. Every penny was put to good use.

As a crane operator my dad taught me pride in honest work. The $5 a week my mother earned cleaning homes reminded me that times were not always good.

They were the pioneers of the life I am blessed with today.

Until a six-year bout of cancer confined her to bed, my mother found purpose in work in her struggle for life. In her suffering she taught me prayer as she clutched her rosary daily.

My parents' comfort came last. They knew how to live with roots firmly grounded in values. My parents knew well who they were. Their generation found little time to identify crises. Narcissism and neglect were unknown to their times. Care and compassion were always in abundant supply.

With their neighbors, they knew they produced a land of peace and plenty. They gave us strong family ties. They took time for people and for God. We are all better for their generation. Thanksgiving is in order. They secured serenity in troubling times a day at a time. They lived the Serenity Prayer, it seemed.

## Moms

A mom's lingering aroma is warm, welcoming and wise. My mom was wonderful, especially when my two brothers, five sisters, and at times, Dad, would wander and lose our way not to mention our straying dog, Chipper.

My mother, deceased since 1975, was more than kind and polite — the way one expects. Being kind and polite is good and makes us feel caring and sensitive to others.

Like a good friend, a loving pastor, or a special neighbor, their spirit lingers long. The aroma of their memory makes many moments. They are special!

Their lingering love, however, is more than kind. Their love, like a hard, long talk with an estranged one, is more than "just mom," "just rich," "just a special neighbor." "*Just them*" is not enough. It is too dependent on one's self (ego), one's personality. *Just them* is not big enough, abundant enough like the many mansions (rooms) in God's house for us! None of that is large enough to expose one to the Easter Christ who is bigger than "just me" and beyond life and death that he conquers!

Zeal, care, dedication, hard work, passion and conviction are often only signs of insecurity or immaturity in Christ. Ego (self) is insufficient for the believer. Believe me, my "ego" gets in the way.

Moms seem to offer the way that is bigger than themselves,

bigger than ego. A mother's ability to "take it or leave it, go with the flow" non-obsessive way keeps mom from too much self-ego. Her way is Christ. Mom's tranquil nature welcomes and warms like that of Jesus' ways that *are* wise! Three cheers for moms and then some!

## Mother's Magic

A mother's work never ends. "Working mothers" became a trendy cry some decades ago, yet, I never knew my mother as ever *not* being a *working mother.* My mom would say that often in her pauses between washing, ironing, cleaning and cooking for the nine of us at home.

Mom could kiss a hurt and make it well almost immediately for one of the four of us in diapers, I was told by Dad. Mom would go to sleep after waiting up long into the Johnny Carson show for one of her children to come home. Mom's magic could fix almost anything — especially broken feelings. Mom could hug us back to health. At Mom's prompting, Dad would lead the parade of us in our two-mile stint to church on a Sunday afternoon. Mom taught me my beside prayer and blessing.

Late into the night, she'd sew our socks and pop the corn and briefly rock in her favored chair. Mom's magic could stretch three pounds of hamburger for nine hungry mouths. Her sizzling apple pies could tempt the kids two blocks away.

Moms today have changed. But the magic of Mother's Day established by congress as a national event in 1913 has not. The idea for Mother's Day, originated by Anna M. Jarvis in West Virginia, had the mark of affection. Although not a mother herself, Ms. Jarvis gave reason for a pause in moms' work that never ends. And, Mother's Day magic gives us the excuse to say, "I.O.U. so much, Mom!" As Julie O'Brien has expressed so beautifully, "Mother, the world may never know that you cared more, gave more, shared more, and loved more than ever was expected. But, Mother, I know."

## Fathers Need to Show Their Sensitive Sides

Faces of fathers express many feelings. Fathers may project anger or aggressiveness, affection or affirmation, appreciation or acceptance. They may be brutal and destructive or spontaneous and playful. But contrary to society's molding men into cold, distant, rugged individualists, fathers need to be uncompromising in disclosing emotion.

The unemployed father, for example, oppressed by bills he cannot pay, is told to keep a "stiff upper lip." Too often society says that if he released that tension, seeks counsel or shows any sign of emotion, he is weak.

We need fathers who feel as fully as humanly possible to create warm and tender relationships with families. Jesus blends the feminine and masculine qualities that psychiatrists affix to each of us. In his assertive moments, Jesus indicts the Pharisees seven times calling them "hypocrites," "brood of vipers and serpents." He says they're like whitewashed tombs that look handsome on the outside, but inside are full of dead men's bones and every kind of corruption.

But traits commonly associated only with women also are fostered by Jesus. People were bringing little children to him, for him to touch. The disciples turned them away, but, when Jesus saw this, he was indignant and said to them: "Let the little children come to me; do not stop them."

The almost-maternal Jesus speaks when he says: "Come to me, all you who labor and are burdened, and I will give you rest." Accepting the tough "macho man" image portrayed by society and blending it with the ability to disclose feelings may find families tomorrow, Father's Day, truly set free.

## Dad's Day

Dad's Day Sunday stops me in my tracks. Father's Day pauses me to ponder my own dear ole dad who grew up in Michigan's Thumb, in Port Austin before landing a job at the Budd Company on Detroit's east side. Born in 1916, his 67 years began with trauma at six-months-old. His birth mother died of tuberculosis, his father remarried and abuse sprinkled through his tale of travail early on before marrying and giving birth to seven children.

A fruitful life of virtue and strength he demonstrated, such as commitment, loyalty, and walking quickly south on Van Dyke from our two-story aluminum-sided, home near Lynch Road, not far from the Detroit City Airport on French Road and Connor, where we often parked on Sunday evening and watched airplanes land and launch.

Dads these days are changing from the rugged rangers who were protectors and providers of families before the Industrial Revolution saw fathers leave the "mentoring" of sons on tractor and farm for the office and the urban adventure and development, and some say, the demise of authentic father-son bonding.

Although I did not always relish the long walks of a few miles from home to Miller and Van Dyke where the parish school and church were situated, the procession of the nine of us stringing along that main street provided time to talk, if not to quicken the pace and catch up to the rest of the clan in route to Saint Thomas the Apostle Church. Riding the bus motivated me more than the hike.

Then there was supper after chores were completed. Unless a good excuse dispensed us from this daily ritual of dining together nightly, we were there reporting on the day's events. Dare any of my twin sisters or brothers mention they were caught cheating on a test or copying someone else's homework. Such confessions would only double penalties with "grounding" or no popcorn at night while we gathered in the living room to watch television or watch mom mend socks or hurt feelings. Dad rested on the couch as he gained energy for his night job at Plymouth Gear and Axle, a block from our house.

None of us would think of missing supper. That ritual had us reporting about the day's events. Through such "town hall" meetings of sort, we worked out differences, and hatched some dreams also, I imagine. Some yelling at times, spilt milk, and insufficient pieces of pie once or twice, kept us knit and supportive.

Having farmed most of his teen years, dad, like mother who grew up on a farm in Cheboygan were "ole-fashioned," and they liked it that way despite our misgivings and protestations about getting home before dark. When my dad was unable to mentor or guide my brothers and me, given his weekend binges on alcohol, there was Fred at the monument company who dropped a pearl of wisdom while washing a grave or tomb stone marker, or there was Father Ed Popielarz, (affectionately dubbed, Fr. Pops) who was quick to encourage, inspire or point out something positive about something I wrote or said. My own dad and these "male mothers" if you will, warned when a road taken was a dead end, or, trying an inexperienced way of doing something was wrought with failure or pain.

While it seems today that men and dads enjoy inclusion, influence and eventually intimacy of "getting close" in sharing significant stuff of life, a father's role is in flux. That gives me reason to appreciate the sturdy and ole-fashioned virtue that anchor me to this day, whether commitment, hard work, or, having learned to walk swiftly in what seemed to be a procession to church for faith that flourishes to this day. Like "rites of passage," initiation, and dark nights or enlightened days, my dad taught me much despite his own human frailty. We're better for it.

Grateful for what he gave me, I'm cognizant that no man, no father is without flaw, failing or frailty. Even in that, I learned something. I rest in knowing that only math and God are perfect. Fathers aren't finished yet, still being formed in the crucible of daily living.

At the end of the last century, only fifty some percent of homes had a dad residing, while at the beginning of that century, over eighty percent felt dad's physical presence. A dad in the house helps, however he may be, the research shows. Homes will only get fixed when we repair and restore a father's place. Fix this problem, we must; however, or its effect will continue to shake the foundations of this land of the free and home of the brave.

### Helpful Suggestions to Deal with Depression

As we enter Holy Week and identify with the passion of our Lord, Jesus Christ, it is an appropriate time for us to also identify with the 17 million Americans with depression. Melancholy moods initiate "down" times with a rhythm of its own. Hard as depression may be, one is more than his or her depressed feelings.

Jesus' own words of seeming abandonment on the cross have him crying out in a way that all humans may identify with – in their good-byes, losses, divorces, tragedies, betrayals, denials and separations (including moves from a home, neighborhood, workplace or school).

Symptoms of depression include diminished interest in social events, changes in sleeping and eating patterns, restlessness or slug-gishness, fatigue, difficulty in making decisions, feelings of worth-lessness and thoughts of death or suicide.

Depression paralyzes people. They chose to do nothing. They avoid others. A loss of confidence and esteem often dominates.

In physically confronting depression, one may try a variety of ways of walking. Positive distraction may help. Breathing deeply aids one in numerous ways. When in a negative pattern, one can do anything positive to break the hold, look at nature, smell a flower, drink some water, take a ride on a bicycle, write in a journal, jot down a poem, say a prayer.

Doing physical things does just that. Refuse to be stuck. Move! Activity and expression may well be the opposite of depression. Being actively involved diminishes depression: cook, dance, play, paint, sing, act, plant a garden.

When depressed, it is important to have hope. Hope is the assur-ance of knowing that the feeling one has is not forever. It is no acci-dent that hope is a Christian virtue.

Science and meditation are gifts from God. Using them well is important. God's goodness shines through psychiatrists and anti-depressant medications.

Psalm 94 of the Bible encourages a person agonizing with depression: "When I said my foot is slipping, your love, O Lord, supported me. When anxiety was great within me, your consolation brought joy to my soul."

Repeating such words of hope can help to still doubt, enhance self-worth and lessen despair. Like mantras, such writings as the Psalms and the Book of Job can provide comfort.

Dignity and worth buoy a psychologically healthy life. Movement from a negative self-image to a positive one involves acting and thinking differently. When one one's efforts are rein-forced, eventually the better and more positive feelings emerge and new behavior results from changed thinking.

Negative thoughts can become negative habits. At its worst, negativity leads to addictive behavior such as drug abuse, overeating, alcoholism, smoking, compulsive gambling, sexual dysfunction and workaholism. These weigh a depressed person down deeper.

Practicing affirmations and validations are helpful. Endorsing one's self, changing negative thoughts to positive ones and lowering unreasonable expectations, all serve to enhance worth and well-being.

Finally, gathering with people who are supportive and positive is key to recovery from depression. And exercise as simple as a daily walk aids a person's emotional state. When walking, alone or with others, stand tall and put your shoulders back, and you'll begin to feel better.

With the wide variety of therapies available today, depression need not be left untreated.

These helps and hints for dealing with depression, a condition that interferes with relationships, work, family and school, are the beginning steps in a healing process.

Most important of all for the depressed person is the knowledge that he or she can recover in time, that there is hope. Treatment is available. When a person is depressed, seek help.

### Love is Tough but Having None Is Worse

A couple of sad parents told me of their daughter's attempt to take her own life. They wondered how it was possible that their daughter could hate herself enough to end it all.

"The doctor straightened us out on love," the father said, "Love is not enough. You have to be your own person." These parents learned about love the hard way. For years, this daughter played the role her parents expected. That was the only way she thought she could get their love. At last, perhaps due to her suicide attempt, they understood the most valuable thing she recovered was her self, her own individual life. No longer would she have to live up to her parents' expectations. No longer would the price of love cost her uniqueness.

Love, I thought, is the most difficult way to live. If it weren't for love, one would not worry about his or her actions and how they affect loved ones. If it weren't for love, one would not worry about losing a job and what that would mean to family.

Parents wouldn't worry about their high school senior out at a parry two hours after the scheduled "due-home" time. People wouldn't have to worry about whether they did all they could for terminally ill loved one. Parents wouldn't spend time hoping and praying that their slow-learner child makes it into the next grade.

I can't think of anything more painful than love and Jesus' command: "By this shall all people know that you are my disciples, that you love one another as I have loved you." (John 13:35). No, I can't think of anything more painful than love – except the thought of its absence, and, that of serenity each day.

## We All Stumble Along Footsteps of the Lonely

She could have been any one of the fifty-seven percent of church members who are single. She wanted to hear something about being single and divorced, widowed, or separated.

Each of us is born alone and dies alone. In between we stumble along the footsteps of lonely literary prototypes such as Abraham, Ulysses, and Faust. Jesus himself was only acting out this basic truth of human life when he forsook the safety of family, friends, and the ties of small town life to live amidst enemies and die deserted by followers.

The first thing about being single is that no one should seek to escape solitude. Solitude ought not to cause one to grab for any and all relationships. Be careful when one feels more himself in the presence of others than when alone. For the single Christian, there is more to affirm than solitude. One must love himself as one made lovely through Christ. Said Sigmund Freud, "It's a good thing people do not love their neighbors as themselves. If they did, they'd kill them."

It boils down to how to love self. It is imperative to be good to yourself when things are going badly. How can we love others without loving ourselves? Love is the gift of oneself. How can one make a gift of that which is hated? But mark the difference between loving yourself and being endlessly preoccupied with self-worth. Narcissists are insecure. Everyone is supported by memories important to his or her personal life. And there is the community of the church. Paradoxically, it is in church that we learn how to live alone – to be free, strong, and mature.

There's an interesting relationship between being alone and in community, "Let him who cannot be alone be aware of community....Let him who is not in community beware of being alone." When apart, we should remember the words of the psalmist, "Wait on the Lord. Be of good courage and He shall strengthen your heart. Wait, I say on the Lord."

*Surrender:*
*Down low as low can go, I "give*
*up" to You! Now, I think I finally get it! Only in You will I turn*
*and be glad all the days of m y life.*
*O Sweet Surrender take my place*
*Untraveled 'til in the arms of my Creator!*
*Come, Surrender, come!*

# CHAPTER SEVEN

# Taking As He Did This World As It Is, Not As I Would Have It.

## My Christmas Tree

Take me; take me, the Scotch pine tree seemed to shout out at me, grabbing for my attention Christmas Eve morning as I scoured the lot for a real tree.

You're crooked, I thought, without hurting the tree's feelings.

Crooked? The tree questioned. What's that, the bent over top of the tree yelled.

Not wanting to give any more energy than necessary, off I went assessing the greenery for the perfect tree.

Ten were still bound tightly and would take a few days for their limbs to loosen. Back I went to the crooked tree.

You again?, it shouts. Yep, I said. Take me, take me, please!, it repeated.

Nothing's perfect but God and math, I recalled. So...please toss it in my trunk, I asked the salesman. Sure will, he affirmed. And I paid the seven dollars and learned a lesson. In a culture of denial, anger, and perfection, Teresa, my just-named crooked tree was perfect the way God made her. Who am I to say what's crooked and what's not? Anyway, Wolfgang, my 4-legged Bichon Frise wouldn't be so rude as to even think Teresa was Crooked. Perfect to

me, he'd bark. Perfect.
Amen.

## Lent, a Time to Repair from Within

How narrow the gate and constricted the road that leads to life, and those who find it are few. Matthew 8:14

In a culture and an economy built on bucks, taking stock of the American way of life is minimal. A busy and frenetic pace each day fails to include pause to reflect and recreate weary bodies, broken hearts, and bruised beings in the wilderness of dog eat dog. Waiting for the weekend charts the course for a different routine with rest that ends up with hectic errands and insufficient time.

For Christians, Lent affords the excuse to enter that narrow gate where few go. That narrow gate is the place and the pause within to let go of the "hold" the American way of life puts on people. A 40-day period of fasting, prayer and acts of charity and love, Lent, from the Old English "lencten," means "springtime."

The "hold" and oppression, coupled with an age of anxiety can be lightened this lent by learning how to live in a new place, a new yard if you will, to rebuild from within. Inner work, beyond the 40-hour-a-week pace, invites us to our center where pausing can convert, change, remake, and transfer living out of our ego (self) and "persona."

Lent is a procession, a pilgrimage, a pause of inner healing that moves beyond our own need to fix and patch broken feelings and weary bones. After all, God crafted human beings not human doings.

There within, we face the wilderness of the desert of daily routines and business as usual. There in that special quieted and still space, we battle beasts of destructive behavior, of working too hard and too long, of shadows and secrets unfaced ever before.

Such transformation and change will not occur; however, unless we learn to wait and be patient. The "Fast food" approach that Americans devour will not do for this inner work. Here, in calm, sin, and the likes of fears and evil are quieted and changed, hearts are enlarged, and life is fuller than the usual fare of each day's brutal beatings. Frozen hearts are thawed to relate anew. Abundant life pervades.

All the cosmetic makeovers, the primping to build bodies with tone and muscle, mean much more in this "inner work" now. Such work is deeper, with depth beyond good looks and skin-deep only humans.

Inner and outer match. They are one. Life is lived differently than where our best thinking has gotten us today, as they say in the 12 steps of Alcoholics Anonymous. Real men and women, outstanding leaders, parents, and others spring from the crucible of going within to "let go" and to be again as originally intended by the Maker.

Ego goes. A nation rebuilds from within, one person at a time. Welcome Lent!

## Jim Carrey in Movie, Me, Myself and Irene Mocks Mental Illness Sufferers

Mental illness is not the stuff of comedy. Jim Carrey as Charles and Hank, who forget to take their medicine for multiple personality disorder in Me, Myself and Irene, is the movie about an ordinary citizen, a Rhode Island State trooper. Without his prescription drug, his two sides vie for the affections of Irene who is confused by his behavior in the relationship.

True genius this film is not. Bawdy, yes. Brilliant, forget it. I was taught that art is meant to make me a better person. This flick only offends and mocks mental illness, a condition that affects one in four American families, and is described by the National Alliance for the mentally ill as a "group of disorders causing severe disturbances in thinking, feeling and relating."

Why shouldn't I laugh at this latest Carrey comedy? Because it is hard enough for sufferers of mental illness to tell their stories and get help to come out and face their struggles. Popular misconceptions about mental illness and Hollywood's depiction of it don't encourage those afflicted by this disease. It locks them further into isolation and despair, even death for some who are overwhelmed by the exclusion, abandonment and names they're called by those who should know better, including Hollywood.

I know of the anguish of mentally ill persons. In counseling them, I hear their cry for meaning, purpose and hope. They wonder if God loves them when they're told that God's love for them is mirrored by their community's care for them. In a depression and believers group I lead weekly, for example, participants relate experiences of others demanding that they "snap out of it" and just forget about their plight. "It's all in your head!"

When statistics show that at least one percent of the American population is diagnosed with schizophrenia or schizo-affective disorder, one thing suffers don't need is another video that pokes fun at how one behaves in multiple personalities when they don't ingest their medication in a timely fashion.

People don't choose to be ill. When genetics and chemical imbalances point increasingly to the causes of one's sickness, reducing one's ailment to choice, character defect, lack of moral discipline and the like only perpetuates the stigma that pervades public thinking.

Multiple personality disorder is hardly a laughing matter. The trauma of sexual abuse in a child, for instance, creates coping mechanisms in which a child may engage a form of dissociation by leaving her body so that the abuse happens to the body but not the mind. This ability to dissociate is key in keeping her from going crazy. The most severe form of dissociation is that in Carrey's character, Charles, who is immersed in anger and rage about something from his past perhaps so much so that another personality is crafted and Hank enters the picture to contend with the highly charged emotion. Feelings of fear have such victims of multiple personality disorder thinking they're crazy. They don't need another film eliciting laugher at their behavior that is totally involuntary.

Individuals, systems and Hollywood need to bring people out of their repression of such denial that trauma, like sexual abuse even happened. Stuffing it only compounds the problem for the victim, family, friends and coworkers.

Long ago I learned that how one behaves is not the issue; rather, how I respond to it is everything. An environment of acceptance helps the mentally ill cope with the terrifying world of shame and fear that is often felt. Concern, counseling, support groups, encouragement and education can diminish the emotional upheaval, feelings of being overwhelmed and practical problems brought on by living with a person who is ill and whose behavior is often difficult.

Even in the so-called modern era, some people still hold that people manifesting signs of mental illness are possessed by evil spirits. They are shunned and called "crazy." Most mentally ill persons are not violent as many still seem to think.

Eradicating myths about mental illness can save lives and offer hope. Films like Me, Myself and Irene only hurt the advances made in research for a cure, along with families, friends, ministers and medical personnel who do a world of good providing skills to manage mental illness. Acknowledging mental illness and addressing it is the only way out of this terrible tunnel. Laughing at sufferers in comedy is offensive. Helping those hurting and watching them heal brings smiles to all.

**Suffering, Stigma, and Church's Role in Preventing Addictions**

Suffering is a fact. How one faces suffering is what matters most, however. St. Thomas a' Kempis, for example, wrote in *The Imitation of Christ*: "The cross always stands ready, and everywhere awaits you. You cannot escape it, wherever you flee; for wherever you go, you bear yourself, and always find yourself."

Attachments, addictions and desires make one anxious and restless, so why go after them? Perhaps St. Augustine of Hippo has an answer: "Everyone, whatever his condition, desires to be happy. There is no one who does not desire this, and each one desires it with such earnestness that it is preferred to all other things; whoever, in fact, desires other things, desires them for this end alone. . .."

Such saints help an addictive culture confront, rather than deny rampant and destructive behaviors. Our communities of faith can also help. Overcoming mistaken stigmas that drug and alcohol dependency results from moral failure and willful misconduct is a challenge. However, combining "the power of God, religion, and spirituality with the power of science and professional medicine to prevent and treat substance abuse and addiction," is the remedy of Joseph A. Califano, Jr., president of the National Center on

Addiction and Substance Abuse (CASA) at Columbia University, gleaning from its two-year study, *So Help Me God: Substance Abuse, Religion and Spirituality: Why Priests and Psychiatrists Should Get Their Acts Together.*

Like Augustine and Thomas a' Kempis, a Vatican Handbook cites a lack of clear, convincing motivation for life as the reason one uses drugs. Drug dependency is a symptom not a disease, the handbook says, at odds with the social sciences that label alcoholism, for example, a disease with a genetic predisposition. Suppression of drug dependency rests with Governments, the Pontifical Council for Health Pastoral Care, who wrote the handbook for the pope, suggests: The Church wants to intervene in the situation of drug addicts in the name of her evangelical mission; with the aim of letting them listen to the word of the love of God, offering the means to spiritually reach all those who are hit by drugs. John Paul steers pastoral workers to help addicts discover their proper human dignity which the drug has buried, the Pope observes. Global and universal in its nature as "catholic," the guide's approach to treatment and prevention is prophylactic (preventing the dangers, assessing the risks, avoiding baleful consequences and helping people take responsibility for the use), therapeutic (aimed at taking care of treating and curing the sick persons), and social (getting the addict into a culture of support, a community, a church, a sponsor, and a groups to be accountable to).

Treatment does work. While assessing addicts at a rehabilitation center in Michigan as a therapist and spirituality specialist, I have watched treatment work when one's own fears and stigmas attached to substance abuse and addictive behaviors are faced.

Take Butch, for example. Two decades ago, he stopped using and has been clean and sober from alcohol and heroine. "It's all God's grace," he reminds his audiences these days when he inspires others to quit, tells his troubling tale of the past, and manages a construction company, while he enjoys his family and parish community. Regularly, Butch participates in 12 step meetings of Alcoholics Anonymous - the effective self help support group for recovering addicts who break denial and admit "powerlessness" over alcohol and drugs (Step one). When weary that he or she cannot beat the opponent in the wrestling ring, to use a helpful metaphor, the abuser surrenders, like Butch did, "to a power greater than self," namely God. Daily practice of the 12 steps affords addicts a framework in recovery, "to breathe under water," to quote Franciscan priest Richard Rohr, who claims the 12 steps of AA are North America's contribution to spirituality.

Stigma, like that attached to persons coping with depressive and other mental illness, finds its self deep in the minds and hearts of some people who should know better. Stigma has been identified as "the most entrenched obstacle for faith communities or spiritualities to overcome," concludes P. Riccio in Prevention Pipeline. Initial use of drugs or alcohol may be voluntary, however, consensus of addiction specialists today agree that use may all too readily lead to addiction, which is now defined as a chronic, relapsing disease that can be successfully treated. Heart disease and diabetes patients, conditions which may result from years of smoking or poor dietary choices, are encouraged and supported in their efforts to secure treatment, yet, drug and alcohol-dependent persons suffer in isolation daily, despite the good news that addictions can be treated as other chronic diseases, such as asthma, diabetes, and hypertension, reports the National Institute of Health, National Institute on Drug Abuse.

The problem of drug addiction has the attention of the Vatican, in as much as a 200-page manual, Church, Drugs, and Drug Addiction was published in 2001 by the Vatican's Pontifical Council for Health Care Workers. This historic document states that drugs are one of the main threats facing young people, including children, let alone obesity in the United States. "Prevention can be brought about by offering to potential victims of drugs the human values of love and life, illuminated by faith," Pope John Paul II stated in this helpful guide that provides strategies for prevention, suppression and rehabilitation.

This handbook invites the Church community to face drug addiction and make it part of the parish's agenda annually in preaching about it, and in hosting prevention programs. While some pastors seem to fear facing addictive behavior, be not afraid, is clearly the message of the Vatican document. With persuasive moral authority and arguments for teens to avoid drug use, I have never felt such strong support for pastoral workers, catechists, parents and formators in confronting this "grave offense," this handbook warns, borrowing from the Catechism of the Catholic Church. "The priest and the pastoral worker have to make a greater effort in order to be present to the world of drug addicts who, with their rejection of reality or with their way of manipulating it, jeopardize a good number of values and constraints." Passage from death, destruction and dealing drugs to an emergence of the paschal mystery's new life of hope and promise is the road addicts steer as they embrace a fearless, moral inventory (Step four), examination of their conscience and harmful ways of sin, and sharing that written accounting with a trusted confidant or priest (Step five). Daily, the recovered, like Butch, promptly admits wrongdoing, seeks forgiveness, and practices this process (Step ten). Unlike the intense "dark night of the soul" of the fourth step's grueling and candid examination, step ten affords one to live in peace with the gift of the present moment. Such calm is met with "conscious contact" with God (Step eleven) through prayer, sacraments and meditation. A deepened resolve for solitude replaced the compulsive, obsessive past in Butch's once staggering saga of self-defeating behavior.

What Butch, and all serious believers, for that matter, let alone addicts feel for the first time, are the three movements or conversions of the purgative (taking off the masks one dons to gain acceptance, uncovering), illuminative (discovering of God's love in its original beauty), and unitive (recovering) union with the Divine Psychotherapist, namely God, who alone heals in one's cooperation with God's grace, favor and blessing on the pilgrim's path. The thirst for God (Psalm 42) beyond artificial means is realized here.

Like Butch, those who know the ravages of nicotine, alcohol, process addictions, such as gambling and work, the quest is quenched as St. Augustine said earlier, when one rests, simply "hangs out" with God, soaking like a sponge in Love. Simply being with God, doing nothing, pervades renewed humans in Christ.

Among other reasons faith communities must overcome stigmas and get involved in this epidemic, reports the U.S. Department of Health and Human Services Administration, Center for

Substance Abuse Treatment, Alcohol, Tobacco and Other Drug Abuse: Challenges and Response for Faith Leaders, include:

For 6 out of 10 Americans, religious faith is the most important influence in their lives, and for 8 out of 10, religious beliefs provide comfort and support; People who actively participate in an organized religious or spiritual group have a great deal of respect for their leaders, who function as teachers, mentors, confidants, as well as advisors. Spirituality is an important part of recovery for individuals with drug and alcohol problems.

Ministries can actually prevent drug and alcohol use by reaching out to youth and getting them involved in positive activities. They can also provide a safe haven for children who are living with drug and alcohol problems at home. Faith can serve as a catalyst for changing public perceptions about addiction and increasing awareness about the good news that recovery is possible.

Additional CASA research shows that:

Teens who never attend church are twice as likely to drink, more than twice as likely to smoke, more than three times more likely to use marijuana and binge-drink, and almost four times more likely to use illicit drugs than teens who attend religious services at least weekly; and,

Teens who do not consider religious beliefs important are almost three times more likely to drink, binge-drink, and smoke, almost four times more likely to use marijuana and seven times more likely to use illicit drugs than teens who believe that religion is important.

Studies show that no area of the country is untouched by addiction. Help is available, however. Treatment works and recovery is possible. Treatment worked for Butch. It works today. Facing addictions and exposing secrecy, sin, and one's shadows (dark, unwanted addictions) to Light is key to unlocking denial and restoring a lost soul's dignity. Enabling the stigma attached to substance abuse by concealing or evading the epidemic proportion only furthers fears and discomforts in talking about the problem, preventing faith communities from healing and their right to treatment and recovery. Dialogue is vital. John Paul's handbook has it right for our Catholic communities when it comes to facing the demon of a culture of addiction.

As St. Thomas a' Kempis and St. Augustine provide assurance that one's heart is restless until it rests in God, and that the way of the cross and suffering will always be part of life's journey, so all of the People of God can be proactive in preventing addictions that continue to skyrocket, in particular. Currently, research shows that 18 million suffer from sexual addiction in the United States and Canada, with cyber addiction escalating each day. To do nothing is to live in denial.

Pope John Paul II's manual on substance abuse is a clarion call to overcome the stigma of addiction, and heralds the importance of spirituality in prevention and treatment. Everyone wins. The evergreen virtue of hope prevails.

## Hearing Children's Cry

Once upon a time there lived a duck called Quack. A checkerboard blue ribbon tied about her neck, made the ceramic, white glazed duck attractive. There on the table sat the duck, proud and proper. Quack longed for visitors and friends. Quack would hope that each time the doorbell rang a new young friend was looking for Quack. Quack waited and waited,

One day the pastor of the church where Quack lived invited the kids over for some stories, Bible stories, duck stories, and a procession-like story in which the kids looked for Jesus while Quack awaited their return to the activity center. The seven smiling faces were thrilled about the stories they would hear and the walk they took looking for Jesus. First, the pastor asked them to draw their home where they live. Then, they printed their names in big bright letters bold enough for all to see. One by one the kids told each other their names. Each said something about their home, the shrubs in front, the pretty red and yellow tulips, the windows wide open and the chimney with smoke rising. Some homes had as many as nine people inside. "Mine's a big family," one little girl yelled with a spark in her eye. "Mine has four," another shouted out. Each clapped for the others after they said their names and showed their houses. In turn, each smiled when their name was said. Clapping filled the air, and hearts swelled with joy.

"Once upon a time," the pastor began, "there was the story told of the duck who had no father." As he held close the duck, all the kids watched eagerly, "But everybody's got a father" one little girl said in the story. She contradicted the teacher and the refrain that repeated "but the duck had no father."

"What should we name the duck?" the pastor asked. "Quack" one bright-eyed boy screamed. "Quacker," another child uttered. They settled on Quack.

"What do you have when you put a bunch of quacks in a box, the story teller asked. "A box of quackers," a lttle one responded.

"If everybody's got' a father," the pastor asked, "who's your father?" "God," the answer came quickly. Right,' the pastor said. "Where's God?" he asked, and one little guy pointed to the cross with Jesus on it that was on the wall. "Where else is Jesus?" the teacher questioned. "In church," came another answer, "Good, very good," said the pastor. "Let's go find where else Jesus may be." They all rose and began their procession in single file, looking for Jesus.

Sister was in the chapel getting Holy Communion from the tabernacle where the consecrated hosts are stored, Sister explained to the little darlings that Jesus was in the tabernacle and that she was taking Jesus to an elderly person in a nursing home. "Jesus also lives in our hearts," the pastor said, pointing to his own heart.

Now," the pastor said, 'where does Jesus live?" "In our hearts, on the cross, in the church, and in the tabernacle," came the answers. "Where else does .Jesus live?" the A volunteer was typing in art office nearby. "Does Jesus live in her?" the pastor asked. All the heads nodded with a smile. Then they went outside looking for Jesus. They went to the school and there the principal met them at the door. "Hi" she said. "What are you doing?" she asked, stooping low to greet them. "We're out looking for Jesus," they said.

"Where is Jesus?" Sister asked. 'in our hearts," they stated. 'That's wonderful, the principal quipped, and off they went to meet the custodian and director of religious education. 'We're looking for Jesus" they said, as the janitor beamed in his blue uniform. "I talk to Jesus every day,' he said, in a hurried state, moving furniture the director of religions education waved goodbye as the procession moved to Mrs. Donley's class.

## Kids!

They run! They fall. They skate board up walls and over curbs. I gotta wonder. What makes 'em move and run and fall and rise only to fall from a wall, a staircase, a curb?

Who knows?

In times when youth find it difficult to create their own healthy activity and games like my generation did, my thoughts turn toward kids this summer.

What will they do with their time? With their health? With their lives? With each other? With their parents?

Least I can do is encourage a young person this summer.

Inspire them. Talk with them. Admire their energy, if anything at all.

Say a prayer for their safety. Smile at 'em. We're all they have, you know!

## Mr. Dunkin's Hole

Once upon a time there lived in Tinsel town, the happily married Mr. and Mrs. Dunkin. Typical home in the land of the free and home of the brave.

Mr. Dunkin desired a Hummer to pull his lawn care equipment. No cheap car there that Hummer be! "Pricey!" his wife screamed, when he arrived home with it one beautiful, bright sunny day. Mrs. Dunkin burst Mr. Dunkin's bubble of joy.

Enraged that Mrs. Dunkin would challenge his prudence, Mr. Dunkin flies off the handle, yells back, and, no longer do they live happily ever after in Tinsel town.

"I deserve a good vehicle." Mr. Dunkin protested. I'm not going to drive a car that breaks down on me!" Fact was, however, that ever two years he wanted a new car. This time, however, a Hummer, put his wife through the roof.

You see, Mr. Dunkin had a hole to fill. No, not in his yard, well, yes, a hole in his pocket. He just couldn't save or see money to pay off credit card debts, and the like. A Hummer, it had to be!

Mr. Dunkin had a hole in his soul. All his life, he told, was filled with rejection and alienation. His was a tale filled with "put downs" and issues with esteem. Early on, in his growing years, he recalled how he was given "nothing" by mom and dad. That angered him. Still does forty years later after drug dependency, and a host of problems.

Now, Mr. Dunkin tries to fill the void in his life and the lack of meaning, with a Hummer. Oh, sweet Hummer heal my hole, he seemed to hope.

Mr. Dunkin's issue is abandonment and anger from his family of origin. A big hole looms large in his life. His agent to fill that lack is spending, buying, shopping 'til he drops. At least, until he gets that Hummer for work. His Hummer feels good for moments, even numbs the pain and heartache of his early childhood rearing. Negative consequences and deeper debt follow his addictive cycle. Finally, diminished self worth has Mr. Dunkin feeling like nobody, nothing at all, like Aldonza in Man From La Mancha.

Mr. Dunkin repeats this cycle of destruction until he changes, or stops, or, says "Enough!" The deep hole in Mr. Dunkin's soul hardly gets filled with a new Hummer. He only wants more. It takes more as his tolerance increases. Like the alcohol dependent person, or the work dependent person, the gambler, the food or sexaholic, the demand for more to fill the hole increases daily until the addictive process stops. If nothing changes, nothing changes!

## Love, Love, Love, Love

Love, love, love, love…So the story says of a monk's retreat at which he uttered the word, love, for the duration of his opening conference. That simple! Love!

Could it have been that was what Mother Teresa was attempting to convey in her interview with William Buckley on *Firing Line* in 1969? In a world of noise, over stimulation by words and the "wild" of an often anxious world in need of healing the wound and hole in its soul, was not Mother Teresa's simple stillness and silence something that attracts the busy bodies consuming and producing so often without the discipline of taking time each day to be quiet?

Call it centering prayer, solitude or mediation — are they not necessary in our addictive society where "doing" and "making money" find us empty with a hole to fill, a void to soothe, a wound to heal from such meaningless activity that does not stem from silence, the mother of Truth? Mother Teresa seemed to pass right by Mr. Buckley when he kept asking her if he could have an address where contributions should be sent for her Missionary Sisters of Christian Charity whose ministry is touch lives with God' love.

*Take, God, receive*
*my all, guiding me to*
*accept You and your*
*path. Still me sufficiently*
*to stop trying to change,*
*control and manipulate You*
*and others with whom I*
*share this planet You made.*

# CHAPTER EIGHT

# Trusting That He Will Make All Things Right If I Surrender To His Will

## I Have a Dream

I have a dream.
I have a dream that we will be God's servants and lift up life (Is.48).

I have a dream that truth pressed to the earth will rise again.

I have a dream that the protection by law for an eagle's egg will be afforded to a baby residing in his or her mother's womb.

I have a dream that with John the Baptist I can say: "And I myself have seen and testified that this is the Son of God (Jn. 1:34).

I have a dream that residents in the womb will be given human and civil rights guaranteed persons living outside the womb. I have a dream.

I have a dream that laws governing truth in lending, advertising and medical procedures that are called informed consent will also be enacted to ensure facts and accurate information on abortion. I have a dream that all human beings will make informed, rational and fully conscious decisions regarding abortion and all other issues regarding life's sanctity.

I have a dream that laws requiring information on abortion

reflect these facts:

That one's heart begins to beat one week after the mother's first missed menstrual period. A baby has its own unique blood type and independent circulatory system.

That one month after the mother has missed her initial period; the baby's brain waves can be recorded and measured. Brain waves are compelling evidence that life is still present in trauma cases. Once recordable brain waves are absent, the patient is declared clinically dead. If the absence of recordable brainwaves declares the end of life, why doesn't the beginning of brain waves signify the beginning of life?

That 12 weeks after conception, through ultrasound imaging, the baby can be observed breathing amniotic fluid by the expansion and contraction of the chest movement of the diaphragm.

That ultrasound depicts infantile movement eight weeks after conception. Motion like a swimmer is noticed about the baby in her or his fluid environs in the womb.

That pain was evident in the Dr. Bernard Nathanson's documentary video, "Silent Scream," in the ultrasound of a 12-week old baby experiencing an abortion. Dr. Nathanson was so horrified by what he had done that he stopped performing abortions ever again.

That according to the Patient's Bill of Rights approved by the American Medical Association (AMA), the patient is told the entire truth, coupled with the dangers of abortion, including sterility, ectopic pregnancy, future miscarriages, and premature deliveries and death from infection.

Yes, I have a dream that these medical facts give life to the Life in the womb once more in the oath of physicians to cause no harm. Amen.

## The Struggle to Save the Soul of the American Family

A vision and plan for family living like Pope John Paul II's 1982 apostolic exhortation, *On the Family,* serves to focus the need for a spiritual foundation in every home. The family needs attentive parents who are appreciative of their children's own needs, gifts and talents, despite the distractions and demons of our day which are vying for the very lifeblood of adults and youngsters alike. A story may help foster the need for constant dialogue in the home where every member is important to the "functional" versus "dysfunctional" family system. A teenager no longer spends time with his brothers and sisters. The usual evening together was replaced by long periods at what has become the American "icon" today, the mall shopping center.

Routinely, as a rite of passage, Joe gathered with his peers each evening in the busyness of shoppers and seekers. One night, Joe's dad decided to warm the fireplace before his son drove off to the mall. "Will you sit with me for a while?" Joe's dad asked. "Sure, Dad, but only for a minute," Joe responded. In complete silence they sat. The fire was watched intently. Finally, fearing that his son would suddenly announce his departure, the father rose to take a hot ember from the fire and put it near the fireplace off by itself. He sat back down and both stated at the lone ember as its warm glow turned ashen gray. The pause pervaded. They pondered.

"I promise to spend at least three nights a week with the family," Joe asserted. I get the picture," he added.

Without explaining, the story points out how a family or any group of human beings, for that matter, is incomplete without each member. A community of persons is impossible without the presence of all. When role models today are reduced to professional sports players or rock stars, the prominent place of parents must be raised again.

Christian parenting in the family is so important and its role is so basic in transforming the world in building the Kingdom of God, that the Vatican Council called it a "domestic church." Only a firm foundation and grounding in God can give parents the tirelessness required in their awesome vocation to create a community of persons. Four ingredients must be included in the way family life unfolds: kindness, compassion love, and a sense of humor.

I remember the words of the late "dean of psychiatry," Karl Menninger, whose lone voice seemed to surface with courage during the turbulent "me" decades since the sixties, when he argued that people need a personal sense of responsibility for moral lapses that leads to their own crippling. In his book, *Whatever Became of Sin?* , his "sin talk" was not stylish for his times; yet, he struggled to help save the souls of the American family by keeping people honest about sin's (and the shadow self's) consequence divisiveness and shame. His love of children as life's greatest natural resource charged parents with their primary responsibility. Menninger said that the way we treat children will indicate the future of society.

The way children have been (mis)treated has to have most Americans wondering about the statistics on the homeless, the criminal young guns, the addicts, and the aborted in our society. Social scientists are suggesting that over half of American families are dysfunctional, or acting out inappropriately by way of an addition to work, drugs, gambling, food, exercise, money, TV, power or sex, to cite some examples.

In order to address the crisis of the struggle for the American soul, one must begin by admitting to a problem if one comes from a family where addictions were present while growing up or currently present. Secondly, one needs to consider therapy and membership in a group such as Adult Children of Alcoholics, AA, or Al Anon. Problems don't get solved alone. Thirdly, being in contact with people who have a similar difficulty helps one recognize and understand how it came about. Fourthly, acquainting one's self with people of similar dysfunction can assist one in changing and becoming more loving. Finally, developing skills to keep one's life in balance can assist in interpersonal relationships.

People without a vision perish, the prophet told. John Paul's *On the Family* points to the importance of a focus for family living. Like a ball park, parameters are necessary within which a family centers its dialogue, attention to one another, discipline, praying and ultimately, acting as a community of persons. A vision provides a purpose for family. With a purpose stemming form the primary models for children, namely the parents, Value-free homes suffer from a lack of direction. Such groping inevitable finds its way into the neighborhood, school, and church. John Paul's exhortation *On the Family* deserves another reading

## A Quiet Revolution Brews Among Catholics

They want answers and accountability. A quiet revolution seems to be stirring among Catholics these days with the daily revelations of priests' abuse of children crisscrossing the country.

Some clergy are ignoring the problem hoping that it will just go away. Younger priests are feeling betrayed by the church they have given their lives to serve. Morale is low. Some priests are waiting for an opportunity to vent their feelings.

People want answers. No longer are they sitting quietly praying, paying and obeying. Crimes have been committed against the most vulnerable among the flocks and parents won't take it any longer.

One Grosse Pointe pastor gathered his parishioners three times to provide a forum for them to address the issue of clergy abuse. At the Sunday liturgies he presented the problem from the pulpit as an extreme embarrassment to the priesthood and a source of discouragement, resentment and anxiety.

The Rev. Joseph McCormack said he wanted to be part of the solution even though he didn't quite know how.

"I feel a responsibility to be part of the solution that can help restore trust, though, I admit, I do not claim to know exactly how to do this," he said, wrestling for a resolution.

Questions surfaced form those assembled at Saint Clare of Montefalco Catholic Church in Grosse Point:

What is your experience of opinion regarding how this issue is being dealt with?"

"Is it being faced square on?

"Is it simply being 'handled?'"

"Is it being minimized?"

Other participants in the speak-up sessions at the parish had other concerns:

"I think the policy of secrecy in the church is very dangerous. We need an open dialogue between the laity and the church hierarchy. The laity have a lot of insight to provide regarding difficult issues such as these."

"My son views this scandal as simply an exercise in institutional self-protection. He concludes that the church, in the hierarchy, is just another self-perpetuating power structure."

"It really bothers me how casually this has been accepted by the church for so many years."

"What did the church hierarchy believe was to be gained by its denial and silence on this issue?"

Tough questions from intelligent parishioners who have a right to answers.

This local pastor took the leadership to tend to his people's concerns and to hear their hurts about the church they love. McCormack listened. He responded as best he could with the information he had. Perhaps it's time for speak-up sessions similar to these.

The problem won't simply go away. Stonewalling and "in house" responses have failed miserably. Someone's "best thinking" got the church to this point. In Alcoholics Anonymous they say: "Our best thinking got us here."

Admission of powerlessness over this problem needs to be embraced.

When issues as important to people's lives as human sexuality are not to be discussed, the repression has to show itself somehow. These unhealthy and criminal manifestations must be addressed front and center. The church's future depends on enlarging the discussion and conversation with the entire people of God.

All of the competencies of the Catholic people need to be engaged in the dialogue in resolving this American issue. Deferring this problem to Rome will no longer sit well with our parishioners. Authentic and honest leadership from the American bishops coupled with their people's input is the only way out. The entire family has to be in on the conversation. Anything less is not fully functioning.

So help us God.

### Making a Difference for Missing and Exploited Children

On June 27th, 2000 our eyes were opened to the enormity of the problem of missing and exploited children. As the parents of a murdered teenager, Molly Bish, who was abducted from her post as a lifeguard, at Comings Pond in the town of Warren, Massachusetts, we learned that teenage girls are at a higher risk for non-family or so called "stranger" abductions, than younger children. We learned that these crimes most often occur in rural-suburban communities, where police often do not have a preplan in existence for when a child goes missing. In fact, if it is a teenage girl they often assume that she has runaway, even when she is a "normal" kid with a stable family relationship.

Prior to June 27$^{th}$, 2000, we thought, I suppose, like most parents in America think; that this will not occur to our family and certainly not in our safe community. It did, with tragic consequences, Molly's remains were found on June 9$^{th}$ nearly three years after her disappearance, about two and one half miles from our home. We were very unprepared for this.

On the first day of Molly's disappearance, the Massachusetts State Police sought our child identification packet on her. While we had one, it was prepared years before, with pictures of her when she was very young and it did not contain fingerprints of her. We found ourselves scrambling to provide the police with the most current picture of her, we could find. These were church, prom, soccer, baseball and other family pictures that were either distant, obstructed or too formal

We learned that parents need to have an integrated child identification packet of their children that includes photos, fingerprints, home video and DNA material. This is easily accomplishedly. It should be done yearly at least. While we all hope no parent has reason to use the "kit", it should be considered part of the continuum of care we all provide for our children.

The availability of a current photo, along with the amber alert, any predator who is bold enough to place our children at risk, while at home, at play, walking with friends or even working, can never be certain that the person in the next car has not observed them and called the police.

I would encourage everyone to support legislation that requires convicted felons to submit to DNA testing. Numerous studies have shown that most violent crimes of rape and murder are committed by repeat offenders and that they have a staircase of escalating criminal activity throughout their lives, that would be prevented through quick and earlier detection and prosecution.

I would encourage everyone to support the president's recent homeland security effort to identify and deport predators, who are illegally living in America. It has always been my fear that Molly's abductor is someone who is transient. These predators know no borders.

We all bear mutual responsibility for our children because they are so trusting. If we all do something, anything, our children, our families will be safer.

Together we can make a difference.

John Bish
P.O. Box 556
West Warren, MA 01090
St. Mary's College, Orchard Lake, MI Class of 1971
Mbish0751@aol.com


**Behold the Lamb of God, Who takes Away the Sin of the World,**
**How Happy Are They Called to the Supper**

Molly, a Lamb of God, innocent, silly and serious saint, poured her blood for the life of many. Like Jesus, Molly was led to the slaughter. Her legacy is long and life-giving. Her inspiration sends her mom and dad and all the communion of saints as an army marching from Massachusetts to Michigan, to Texas and beyond. All speak out, all speak Truth in love to save our children, take them back, and raise them up! Terrorized and traumatized, Molly Bish was kidnapped and killed.

Martyrdom is the supreme sacrifice for the faith. Molly embraced faith in life and death and even now. She sends us with John and Magi, Heather and John Jr., into the streets and cities to protect our youth.

Until the Lamb and the wolf will feed together at the same table in the vision of the Hebrew scriptures, until the kingdom of God breaks forth in fullness, we will fight so that there will be no more lambs and lost lives slaughtered with their blood poured here in America, the land of the free and the home of the brave; in AIDS-infected children and parents in Africa; in the wombs of America; in the government of Pol Pot in Cambodia where millions were murdered; in Iraq and Israel and Palestine; in West Warren, Massachusetts; in the concentration camps of the slaughter of Jews; and , in our own hearts where dragons may dwell, and dragonflies with God's touch will drive away, undo and heal for the harmony of the world, and the well-being of the body of Christ.

Until the Lamb and the wolf will feed together at the same table, we will shout and sing with Isaiah the prophet (Is.65:25):

The wolf and the lamb shall feed together,

They shall not hurt nor destroy in all my holy mountain, says the Lord.

And in another place the same prophet says of his mission, like that of Molly's and moms and dads and Heather and John Jr., and each of us this day and tomorrow when the grief will be great:

To bind the broken hearted,

To exchange beauty for ashes,

The oil of joy for mourning,

The garment of praise for the spirit of heaviness,

That the people will be trees of right,

The planting of the Lord, that he might be glorified.

For as earth buds (and butterflies fly)

And the garden cause the things that are sown in to spring forth so God, will cause right and praise to spring forth before all nations.

With the elder, wise, and sage of old Solomon (Song of Solomon 2:10-13), and with the wisdom to teach our young people about inner authority, Truth, and sexuality, so there will be no more abuse of power in our culture and homes, we pledge this day together, as my Beloved spoke and God says to Molly and mom and dad, and Heather and John, Jr. and me:

Rise up my love, my fair one, and come away.

For Lo, the winter is past, the rain is over;

The time of the singing of birds is come and

The voice of the turtle is heard in our land;

The fig tree puts forth her green figs, and
The vines with the tender grapes give a good smell.
Arise my love, my fair one, and come away.
Yes, come now, all to the table of sacrifice, of slaughter of the
Innocent Lamb, come my lovely one and eat and say:
Behold the Lamb of God who Takes away the sin of the world;
How happy are we called to the supper.

*Gentle Creator,*
*May I accept the reality*
*of pain and violence in*
*our time of terror and*
*trauma. Give me the wisdom*
*to know, O God, that what*
*I can do is prepare the*
*way with love for your healing*
*of our earth's ways.*

# CHAPTER NINE

# That I May Be Reasonably Happy In This Life and Supremely Happy With Him, Forever In The Next

## The Last Word

Eternal Rest for a Good Shepherd
August 3, 1937 – March 27, 2004
Kenneth E. Untener, the fourth bishop of Saginaw, MI, for 24 years before his death March 27th from complications of leukemia, understood connectedness so well he never even had a life of 'his own' in the sense of Frank Sinatra's oft-quoted "I did it my way," concluded Sister Liz Picken, Untener's theological consultant.

Connected he was indeed. This traveling man of God envisioned a wider horizon as shepherd for the 140,000 Catholics in his 11-county diocese. While introducing himself to the diocese in November of 1989 in the civic arena, he said: "I'm Ken, and I'll be your waiter." And serve he did, but, not before grounding his own roots and relationship with God first rising daily by 4 AM. In his inner office, for example, the Scriptures, a lit candle, a scene from a gospel, and a journal script for his popular "Little Books" were born in his contemplative connecting with God. Here, roots ran deep. Solid spirituality seemed key.

When his platter was full on certain days, or required difficult decisions, his prayer ended with, "Lord, I have a loaf and two fishes, but what are these among so many? I trust you will multiply it." Whether working out with the Saginaw Gears, the minor league professional hockey team, or playing the piano at a sing-along, or roller blading on the chancery parking lot before staff reported for work, a culture of support and Vatican II's "Communio" was as essential for Ken as for his mentor, and model with Christ, the missed and much-beloved John Cardinal Dearden, president of the National Conference of Catholic Bishops and former archbishop of Detroit. Dearden, implemented Vatican II with small groups and home "speak up" sessions called, Synod '69, and later hosted the National Call to Action in 1976.

Call it dialogue. Call it servant leadership, and call it "fresh air" of the Holy Spirit. Perhaps his drive and dialogue and culture of connection and motivation stemmed from acceptance of a prosthetic lower right leg. He knew suffering and shortcomings and emerged the "better" for them.

He shared how he went for maintenance on his prosthetic leg and observed a new building with separate rooms for each patient, unlike the once common area where walls didn't prevent peer ministry of sharing. His doctor beamed about the new "digs" but Ken told him he liked the old, common space better.

Connecting also with children was obvious at Mass. One morning Untener the good bishop engaged those assembled with the question: "Who else did Jesus heal?"

"The blind."

"Right, Who else?"

"Lepers."

"Right."

Then a voice midway the church shouted an answer Ken couldn't hear. "Pardon me?" the homilist asked. The young boy said it louder to no avail.

"Who?"

"The deaf," the boy thundered back.

"I have come to believe that my task is to craft something small, something good, that the Master will use," Ken said. Action followed. He built. He knew how to network well. Former religion writer for the Detroit Free Press, Episcopal priest Harry Cook told me that Untener's death is a "huge hole" for him personally, having hosted Ken at St. Andrew Episcopal Church in Clawson, MI., to reflect on the Stations of the Cross one Good Friday.

Cook also told of the time his own bishop, William Gordon of Midland, told his wife, Shirley: "Guess, who is coming to dinner and living with us for a couple of months?"

At Sacred Heart School of Theology in Metropolitan Milwaukee, I remember Untener telling the older candidates studying to be priests to "find a way to pray," and "don't be postage stamp and baseball card collectors. Those you do alone. You need to connect." Sound advice served in a "lone ranger" world - A menu from a man much loved in Saginaw where hearts grieve these days. Wit, humor, joy and enthusiasm flowed from this shepherdly leader who taught by example, who wrote by story, and knew the importance of, and insisted on relational skills building in formation ministry whether at St. John Seminary in Plymouth, Michigan where he served as rector, or, in the ministerial program in his diocese. Untener worried about foundational cracks in candidates for the priesthood or religious life. Flaws and failings were understandable, but he had doubts about personality disorders embedded in one's core being. A practical and concrete pastor, Ken lived and worked in the trenches where his workers ministered. He knew their aches and pains and walked their path.

In God's heart and American Church history is forever etched Kenneth Untener: "Good and faithful servant."

It was a thrill to await Bishop Untener's arrival at parish churches in Caseville, or Ubly, or Port Austin, in Michigan's Thumb, where he was to preside. What I savored mostly was his enthusiasm for preaching, how he seemed to "light up" a crowd and send folks off feeling fed and good about themselves. The table at which he presided made room for all people. Perhaps that's because faith, hope and love, the theological virtues, and fortitude, temperance, justice and prudence, the cardinal virtues encompassed Ken Untener. Once when I was visiting a Capuchin priest in Sanford where Ken was residing at the time (one among the more than 100 rectories, hospitals and other sites he stayed in for 4-6 months and then moved on). Upon returning home one evening, Ken grabbed a Coke, came into the common room, chatted some, then asked us to name the virtues as though he forgot. We both fumbled. I haven't since that night. In fact, I made sure the virtues listed in the Catechism of the Catholic Church (CCC) were included in a talk recently on the widening gap of rich and poor in our land, and the call of virtue in our personal living and choices.

Ken's table had him mandating two decrees at the Cathedral of Saginaw, March 26, 1991: (1) "I hereby decree that wherever and whenever these oils are used, they be used generously," he persuaded that Holy Thursday, and, (2)..."From this day forward until July 1, l991, every meeting - no matter what its purpose shall have as its first agenda item this question: "How will what we are doing here affect or involve the poor?" Untener said that if the poor were central to Jesus, so they must be for the Church, also. His decrees were met with sustained and standing ovation. They were observed also. Research shows the effectiveness of his mandates the day Jesus washed feet before his Good Friday cross. Ninety-seven days of his decrees has his flock talking about the poor as "normal" meeting conversation ever since the experiment began. Comparing the decrees success to Weight Watchers, the bishop said that changing their eating habits is the true measure of success. Jesus as leader for Ken shined June 13th when Untener's theological consultant, Liz Picken, and Bishops Thomas Gumbleton and Walter Schoenherr reflected on the life and legacy of this good shepherd in St. James Church in Novi, Michigan, as the flock still mourned the man's demise.

At his funeral Mass of Christian burial, the retired friend and Archbishop John R. Quinn said in his homily of Ken: "Intelligent, articulate, immensely gifted, he spoke the language of the heart and our heart spoke back."

Controversy didn't scare Untener into silence of sitting down at National bishops' meetings. If they didn't want to discuss human sexuality, he'd remind his Episcopal brothers that they were acting like a dysfunctional family. He established support for pregnant women when abortion was the issue. The Church is most true to its tradition, he said, when it's open and inclusive, speaking about homosexuality.

This good shepherd seemed to know and live the reality that at death the lone thing parishioners will be judged upon is how others were treated.

Until we connect again one day, I will forever relish that Saturday morning I mustered the courage to call Ken weeks before he died. My call was put right through to Ken at the Immaculate Heart of Mary Memory Center in Monroe, MI. With weakened voice we prayed, conversed, and he said "Thanks," when I told him he was fresh air. We prayed and said, "Goodbye."

Eternal rest grant unto him, O Lord, and let perpetual light shine upon him...

## In Dying We live, and in Living We Die

It never fails. Each November my mother Edith comes to mind. Perhaps her six-year battle with cancer, the pain and the promise of her life, and my own moments with her when she finally expired that early Tuesday morning of 1975, bring back these memories. "Please don't take me back to the hospital," Mom told me. "Please, it's so cold there."

She had that right and it was respected. Familiar surroundings were the least that could be given to her, I thought. She had the right not to die alone. The tender care and attention given her by one family member who stayed with her continually spelled commitment and faithfulness to the dying. I knew she had the right to be cared for by sensitive people who understood her needs and would buoy her hopes.

Patient and enduring love finds its place so rarely these days," I said. "What possibly could be more important than the right the dying person has to the touch of human hands on their passing pulse?" Without a doubt, she had the right to have help from her family in accepting her death.

Mom had the right to be listened to, but by then she could not talk. The coma prevented that. I was glad we had shared the memorable moments of her fifty-five years of life, moments of changing diapers for her other children; the celebration of her 25th wedding anniversary, when she danced her last waltz with her husband; the 1968 announcement of her son's death in Vietnam. So much in so little time, I thought. She had the right to celebrate.

She had the right to share in the decisions about her death as long as she possibly could. She had the right to die with dignity, never to be deceived about her fate. I remember a passage from "Little Gidding" by T.S. Eliot: "We die with the dying: See, they depart and we go with them. We are born with the dead: See, they return and bring us with them."

## Leona Nourished Life to the End

My visits were not easy with Aunt Leona, my godmother. With a constant smile and a deep faith in her Maker to support a quickly fading life, Leona recently died of cancer. Until her final breath, she nourished my life by good example — the promise godparents make at Christian baptism. When we talked I heard her gently speak:

"Hear me. Let me speak about how I feel. I see the pain, the worry and the confusion of so many family members and friends. Help them. Travel with them and me together.

Ask my doctor how I am doing. You know I want to know. Be honest, though for me and for you. Death is a part of life. It's real. And it's happening to me right now, much to my surprise.

Help me feel my fears, frustrations, and laments. Please don't talk or pray me out of them. I need to wrestle with these things. Tell them it's okay to be angry at you, the nurses, the doctors, my family, even my God. Treat me not as a patient with the usual hospital routine.

"Don't let the loss of my hair; weight and enthusiasm for life throw you. I know you're threatened by that sudden intruder into my life. Use this opportunity to deal with your fear of dying.

"Touch me. Sometimes I feel as if I have leprosy. Hug me. I also need affection and affirmation, you know. Dignify my dying and don't deny me my God-given worth. Before it is too late, tell me you love me. Let me talk about my story, the farm, the family, the years of laughter, the depression times, the dances and dinners, the trying times and the tears. Remind me of the difference I made to you, the friends, the church activities, the vegetables and fruits Matt and Bobby and I canned together. Pull out of me memories of married life marked with love.

"Please pray with me; and don't hide behind pious platitudes that I can't understand. Help me deal with God when I ask, 'Why me? Why now?' Pray *with* me, not *for me*. I'm still alive, you know.

"Give me eternal rest. Grant me peace."

## Msgr. Clement Kern, Remembered

Passion for the poor and disposed pervaded Msgr. Clem Kern's life and ministry. Quietly, he moved with the mission of Jesus to serve the lowly and bring them to higher places of hope.

Detroit's Most Holy Trinity rectory bustled with activity one afternoon when I visited. God's variety of people wanted to see the monsignor. Busier than a railroad station, Holy Trinity served the sorely needy and the outcast — the folks the Gospels tell us about. The Rev. Samuel Campbell counseled an alcoholic, while Msgr. Kern served a woman in need of food.

Both men strengthened my drive to serve as priest. Little did they know that they were vocation directors encouraging others to dare walk in their footsteps someday. Clem Kern believed in God and the poor. He built up the dignity of a fragile people. When no one else seemed to be there, Clem Kern took up the cause.

He brought a conscience to labor in Detroit. He walked where others chose never to be. Farm workers found him picketing unjust labor practices. Gays saw him lead them in prayer at Mass. He beat red tape and bureaucratic systems. People were more important; their dignity was at stake.

He was an ordinary man with an extraordinary ministry. He was one like many: poor. He was empty enough of this world's ways to fill up on the ideals of the Gospel challenge. When Msgr. Kern was asked why he did what he did, he replied, "The people asked me."

We asked him to be our public examination of conscience. He was that; and, he was more. He was passion for the poor — for all of us — for we are all poor in some way. That's the miracle his memory will provide us. Still, his passion will heal as we remember him well. Blessed among us — a saint!

Rest in peace, Clem!

## Harry Chapin Is Missed

Half of Harry Chapin's annual concerts were benefits, mostly related to the cause of world hunger. The late songwriter's real passion was in moving his audiences to sit up and take a stand on the issues of the day.

"At a time when the music industry seems to have lost its head," Chapin said, "I feel more sure of where I am and where I'm going than ever before. My stance as a storyteller and social commentator is probably more necessary and will be more listened to in this decade than it was in the past one. I'm ready to dream again. Aren't you?"

Chapin's talent was demonstrated by his tenacity to convince former President Carter to form a Presidential Commission on World Hunger in 1976 on which he sat. He helped form an organization called World Hunger Year and a Washington-based lobbying group called Food Policy Center and was appointed to the White House Cambodia Crisis Committee.

The Christian citizen's movement, Bread for the World, also received much support from Chapin, who expressed concern about the political climate and the seemingly callous attitude of people toward the underfed and oppressed, before his tragic automobile death on the Long Island Expressway.

"The real question is whether America is going to use Reagan as an excuse to forget about things that it already knows it should stand up for. When David Stockman says to America that there's no such thing as entitlement, it's giving us all an excuse not to feel guilty about them (the poor) and to just be selfish. We know that's nonsense; because, we know that Nelson Rockefeller, when he was born, was entitled to $400 million and somebody else was entitled to brain damage because of malnutrition. The scary thing about the current political situation is that it is allowing people to have a political excuse to go to sleep."

Harry slept little when it came to the social consciousness

arena. He was hoping that hunger would be disposed of in our time. His song needs to remind us that the hungry are still with us.

And, Harry Chapin's ten-year career, including such hits as "Taxi" and "Cats in the Cradle," needs to continue in personages like Kenny Rogers, Steve and Tom Chapin (his brothers) and each of us. His dream must never die as long as hungry people are around.

## Jackie Set Example for All

They say that the passing of Jackie marks the end of an era. Tell me it's not so. The era of the sixties was a majestic moment of bold dreams daring to lead differently. A freshness pervaded the leadership of youthfulness, vigor, and courage.

The bonding and kinship with the Kennedys signals this nation's need to reclaim the strengths and virtues embodied in Jacqueline Kennedy Onassis — despite her tragic and terrible heartache, hurt, some say hell.

A warm, witty, and wonderful person was Jackie, commentators say. To watch her in the face of the pain that poked so often at her sustained this country's grief at the death of her husband, John. Hers was a gallant and graceful life. Jackie walked through life as a gift for us to emulate. Her virtue is too grand to lose. In her extraordinary life of sixty-four years she was ordinary enough for the common to feel kinship, closeness, communion and connectedness. Although she was from wealth, she was able to attract the very ordinary in her love of words, the arts, adventure, family and friends.

Jackie's quiet presence was watched jogging in Central Park, lobbying to preserve architecture such as the Grand Central Terminal, church-going, reading, and proudly parenting Caroline and John who were robbed of their father so soon.

The poets suggest that no one really dies until you and I die. Jackie's virtues need to be reclaimed by this nation when such strengths are too easily trampled by the violence of other forces less noble - guns, crime, and lack of discipline, family destruction, drugs, and despair.

Just as the torch passed to the leadership of the Kennedy era, that small light can glow long and diminish not. Jackie's was a legacy as she was a legend. She showed us how to do life. We watched and witnessed well. We bonded with her. Hers is too grand, gallant, great and graceful a gift to give up now in her death. May the truth of the torch she lighted be lifted lifelong for little ones and lost ones, wealthy ones, and the poor, the purposeless, and our children who will take on Jackie's common strengths and virtues as they now watch us embody such grace. We can't afford to let the light go out.

## There's No Need to Fear Death

To all things there is a season. Life is wrapped up in nature, and until we learn to deal with death, we are going to live with fear.

In our death-denying culture, discussion on death becomes all the more important for us if we are to revise our attitude toward it and live our lives in hope and purpose. So often, society fails to deal with death as a natural phenomenon but rather as an enemy to be conquered and not realistically faced.

I'm not denying that death causes hurt and can be tragic. We must deal with death as a natural event rather than one that evokes fear and unnecessary suffering.

Someone once suggested to me that we ought to prepare for death in much the same way we prepare for birth. When a child is about to be born, we talk about whether the bedroom should be painted pink or blue; and, if we're not sure, yellow. If we can talk about death the same way, perhaps we would live differently. We would see that life and death are one.

I realize that just as birth and death are personal and family affairs, learning to cope with them begins with parents and teachers. Children need not be burdened with their parents" or society's hang-ups about death or dying.

Children must come to grips with the inevitability of death as soon as they encounter the death of a pet and not be shielded from it because of adult fears. The development of trust in children is important in view of a healthy attitude toward life and death. Webster's dictionary points out that trust, the first of the psychologist Erickson's ego values, is defined as the "assured reliance on another's integrity," the last of Erickson's ego values. Erickson says that healthy children will not fear life if their elders have integrity enough not to fear death.

Case histories may point out the influence that parents may have on children's basic attitudes toward life and death. First impressions are that children and death are poles apart. Death, on the other hand, is still, cold and foreboding. Nonetheless, children ask about the nature of death. What we say will have a lasting impression.

Perhaps one of the basic problems in dealing with death and talking about it is the fact that it is described by so many so differently. Freud, for example tells that it is indeed impossible to imagine our own death because in the unconscious everyone is convinced of his own immortality. Rollo May, on the other hand, asserts that repression of death equals our obsession with it. Violence, sex, drugs, and the occult are obsessions of the time which point to man's need to overcome death, he concludes. Drugs, for example, tend to erase time, to take one out of the time world which marks the steps toward death. Drugs put the user into a zone of free-floating fantasy, psychologists tell us.

I remember a child asking me in class once about why people die. Admittedly, I told her I didn't know but then I went on to talk about her father's car when the engine doesn't work anymore. A comparison of the engine and the person who dies was attempted. The child seemed satisfied for the time being.

Standard responses are often dishonest. Sometimes, the child is told that the dead person is on a journey or just sleeping, or, even, on vacation! Sometimes we get too complex in explaining death to children. Parents may tell children that it is the will of God that the person died, consequently conjuring up an image of God as the "enemy." Good mental health has to do with a serious examination of feelings about death.

Children are often kept from senior citizens who could help the child's awareness of himself and the world. A mutual enhancement could be achieved in schools if senior citizens were given the chance to exchange views with children.

Death in the Christian context can have a tremendous value in the total life of a child's well-being. Fundamental to the child's curious questions is the general Christian atmosphere of trust and acceptance at home and in school. And although the idea of faith cannot be grasped by the child, any mention of death needs to be kept as simple and as concrete as possible. The fact that a flower can die or that a car's engine will break down can make sense to the child. Stable and trustworthy love in the family and school community can help promote a more solid understanding of his life; and, therefore, of his death. We may be able to deny death; but, we can't escape it. It's a very natural part of life.

## Life Starts Being a Gift When You Give it Away

God helps me let God be God and me be me, not God. God gave me all "my" things. Even Wolfgang, my 4-legged Bichon Frise, and my jogging shoes. And my friends. And my food.

God gave me health. I should say God blessed me with health, not my health; not my children, but God's children, of whom I am a temporary caretaker. Not my home, but God's home, of which I am expected to be a wise steward. Not my money, God's money, of which I am to be responsible!

Death turns me on. Funny, isn't that? A healthy person thinking about death. Hmm...

When I think about my own death (rather, the death God will call me to do!), I realize that I take nothing with me when I go. Just me and all my empty promises. All the temporal things behind: time, health, money, property, profession, priesthood. Nothing will I take out of this world.

You know what turns me on? Giving t his away. 'Cause it isn't a gift until I give it away. I want to give my life away. To You. To God. What turns me on is a litany of questions that matter most:

How do I use what God temporarily entrusted to me? (Not so well always; selfishly, also. You, too?) Do my attitudes and actions further the will of God for my short stay on Earth? Was and is God's name glorified? Do I advance God's kingdom?

Commitment turns me on. I learned commitment from my mother, who raised and washed diapers for four of us at one time

(God's blessings of two sets of twins!); and, from my dad (God rest them) who worked three jobs at one time to support us. My grand-mother fed her chickens daily in the rain or in the sun, in the cold, and in the warm. God bless them all! We're called to commitment also (Romans 121-2) God asks for nothing less than a total commit-ment. Life starts being a gift when you give it away

Now is the time.

**"There is a time for everything,
a season for every activity under heaven.
A time to be born and a time to die." Eccl. 3:1-2**

# *Conclusion*

Troubling times filled with terror and trauma require "down" moments when I can be still and quiet.

These tales and tips for securing serenity were born out of decades of desolation and consolation, ups and downs, good and bad days of sorrow and joy, gladness and madness as well. Suffering and sorrow are part of the package of living. All I need do is accept it to move on.

Like the scenery of pastoral greens and golds and browns, the array of moods and moments of living are mixed. The color and texture of life merges to make celebration of living one day at a time worth it all.

Many of these pages were ready in 2002. I was not. A crisis of leadership and lack of passion to provide a safe container for children troubled this soul.

Conditions of our culture put me into a tailspin of wonder, ache, hurt, deep sadness and many moments of confusion.

That "stuff" of life didn't have to be. But, it was reality. I had to accept the sereneless times, but could not.

With unfolding time, trust and conversation around the Table with confident acquaintances, family and friends, those seeming futile feelings surrounding me evaporated like the misty dew of a fresh dawn. A book was born!

The time had come! These serene and not so serene thoughts tugged at my heart, while companions of Care of the Soul (www.CareoftheSoul.org) including Ruthmarie Shea-Atallah, Kathy Hasty, JoAnn Loria, Mary Moore, and Larry Saville, the Board of Directors, encouraged me sufficiently to put pen to paper. Along with Steve Macarthur, Ph.D., a marvelous human being, I was also inspired with the embodiment of serenity and peace in Bishop Thomas J. Gumbleton, and always grateful for his wisdom and words. Dedicated pastors from Detroit and its surroundings are remarkable ministers with the People of God in turbulent times. They remind me that imagination and fun times in the middle of chaos buoys a sad soul, and resolves critical issues in church and society. Together, we make a difference and speak to authority Truth in love. We imagine more than a business and corporation model that refuses to fit Love, and will fail the church until the ancient and revered tradition and "cura animarum" of Pope Gregory the Great's households is appreciated once more and revived. Thanks to Marcee Pajek, Norm Moore, Olga Dudun, Ernie Bedard, Larry Kaiser, Carol Hofer, Jim Scheick, Joanne Simonte, Louis Reuss, Dick Lehmann, John Barkay, Joe Gembala, Don Worthy, and George Charnley for their assistance. To Marcy, Lukas, Marlene, Bob, Diane, Pat, mom and dad, I am most grateful! Thanks to Eveleen Forkin and Marge Hallman, Bob Wurm, Eleanor Josaitis and the late William Cunningham, Don Hessler, and Clem Kern.

Countless other companions enhance the esteem of God's pilgrim people. They help Care of the Soul realize its mission: To ignite each one's dignity and worth by awakening it in self and others. +Blessings on all, on our world, and God bless peacemakers in troubling times of fear and terror that need not be if in Christ.

This heart swells with gratitude. Securing serenity silences my heart to pulsate anew, attuning to the Creator one moment at a time, rising each morning to Louis Armstrong's, What a Wonderful World!

Mother Teresa of India was asked what happened when she prayed. God listened, she said. And what else, the questioner pressed. I listened, she concluded.

Listening is a lesson I need to learn. Leaders need to listen long in troubling times if serenity is secured.